VEGAN MEAT

Plant-Based Guide for Using Meat Substitutes

(Making Vegan Meat, Vegan Cheese and Vegan Fish)

Amaranta Keller

© Copyright 2021 by Amaranta Keller

All rights reserved.

This document is geared towards providing exact and reliable information with regards to the topic and issue covered. The publication is sold with the idea that the publisher is not required to render accounting, officially permitted, or otherwise, qualified services. If advice is necessary, legal or professional, a practiced individual in the profession should be ordered.

- From a Declaration of Principles which was accepted and approved equally by a Committee of the American Bar Association and a Committee of Publishers and Associations.

In no way is it legal to reproduce, duplicate, or transmit any part of this document in either electronic means or in printed format. Recording of this publication is strictly prohibited and any storage of this document is not allowed unless with written permission from the publisher. All rights reserved.

The information provided herein is stated to be truthful and consistent, in that any liability, in terms of inattention or otherwise, by any usage or abuse of any policies, processes, or directions contained within is the solitary and utter responsibility of the recipient reader. Under no circumstances will any legal responsibility or blame be held against the publisher for any reparation, damages, or monetary loss due to the information herein, either directly or indirectly.

Respective authors own all copyrights not held by the publisher.

The information herein is offered for informational purposes solely, and is universal as so. The presentation of the information is without contract or any type of guarantee assurance.

The trademarks that are used are without any consent, and the publication of the trademark is without permission or backing by the trademark owner. All trademarks and brands within this book are for clarifying purposes only and are the owned by the owners themselves, not affiliated with this document.

TABLE OF CONTENTS

Introduction 1

Why Plant-Based Food? 3

Fight Hunger In The World 13

It Promotes Biodiversity And Respect For Nature. 15

It's An Act Of Self-Love. 18

Nutritional Value 20

Improved Mood 21

Disease Prevention 22

Weight Loss 24

Improved Athletic Performance 26

You Won't Give Up Amazing Flavors. 28

Best Delicious Vegan Meat 32

VEGAN PORK RECIPES. 32

    1. Daikon Bacon 32

    2. Thick-Cut Seitan Bacon 35

    3.Bacon From Mochi (Sweet Rice Flour) 40

    4. Smoked Watermelon Ham 41

    5. Grill Mushroom Ribs 46

    6. Vegan Pork Rinds (Fried Rice Paper) 47

    7. Vegetarian Force Pork Sandwich (Bbq Soy Curls) 51

    8. Vegan Pepperoni 57

    9. Sweet And Sour Pork Recipe 64

    10. Guinness Pulled Pork 67

    11. Fiery Pulled Pork 69

    13. Vegetarian Pernil Formula 74

VEGAN CHICKEN RECIPES. 75

    1. Vegan Chicken Nuggets 75

    2. Tofu Orange Chicken 78

    3. Hot Seitan Buffalo "Wings" 81

4. Velvety Vegan Chicken And Rice...84
5. Vegan "Chicken" Pot Pie With Garden 87
6. Vegetarian Tempeh "Chicken" Salad 90
7. Vegetarian Cashew "Chicken" Stir Fry 92
8. Seitan Fried "Chicken" Tenders 95
9. Veggie Lover Chinese Kung Pao Tofu......................................97
10. Orange Glazed Tempeh..101
11. Veggie Sweetheart Moroccan-Style "Chicken" Stew............103
12. Vegetarian General Tso's Chicken 106

VEGGIE LOVER BEEF RECIPES..109
1."Beef" Stroganoff With Veggie Lover Substitute 109
2. Veggie Dear Meat Pie With Plant-Based Meat 111
3. Veggie Lover Impossible Swedish "Meatballs" 115
4.Vegan Southwestern-Style Chili Recipe 118
5. Vegetarian Tvp Sloppy Joes..121
6. Veggie Darling Chili With Smart Ground Mock Meat
Crumbles 123

VEGETARIAN FISH RECIPES..126
1. Tofish And Chips 127
2. Vegan Tuna Sushi Bowl..129
3. Veggie Lover Tofu "Fish" Sticks 131
4. Banana Blossom Fish Cakes..134
5. Veggie Darling Filet-O-Fish Sandwich 136

VEGETARIAN CHEESE RECIPES 139
1.Cranberry And Pecan Vegan Cheeseball..................................139
2. Veggie Lover Parmesan Cheese 141
3. Sound Vegan Queso 142
4. Avocado Cashew Cream Cheese..144
5.Creamy Vegetable-Based Vegan Cheese Sauce.......................145

INTRODUCTION

More than seventy-five years have progressed since The Vegan Society was founded by English animal rights defender Donald Watson and his colleagues, who described and simplified contemporary veganism.

Vegans develop a plant-based diet, which suggests they do not eat meat and do not use or consume animal products. Actors like: Lewis Hamilton, Miley Cyrus, Ariana Grande, and others stick to a plant-based diet. So why do people go vegan?

Scientists say we must immediately eat less meat and change how we manage the land to stop the climate crisis. Doctors, that having a plant-based diet could have multiple benefits on our health and philosophically, veganism gives us the idea of putting into practice a more respectful and empathetic relationship with animals since it is understood that they are sentient beings with the capacity to love, feel and make decisions.

The world of veganism is one full of satisfaction and positive results; but also a challenging one due to a world full of baseless prejudices and access to a world of misinformation.

That is why I was determined to create this book, to help all those who think differently and are willing to take that next step to enter a world full of self-love and the world around them, to have a comfortable transition and enjoy the process. A plant-based diet is not giving up the things we love. It simply consists of transforming habits and incorporating new ways of doing things into our lives.

This book is a guide made with dedication and effort from someone who has already gone through this transition. Here you will find recipes full of nutrients and flavor, which will make you enjoy every day of cooking and the result through simple instructions. You will find the list of ingredients necessary to make each of the exquisite dishes that I have prepared for you, which are easily accessible, with no unknown names! Also, you will learn how to make meat and cheese from scratch because I want to emphasize this again, it is not about abandoning the things you love, but about incorporating them in more creative and healthy ways.

WHY PLANT-BASED FOOD?

What do an email, a bag of chips, and a person have in common? That all of them generate an environmental impact known as a carbon footprint. Every one of us generates a carbon footprint on the planet. This footprint is the environmental impact generated in the development of an activity. How much harm do you think you do every day?

The carbon footprint is the greenhouse gas emissions produced by manufacturing, using, and disposal of merchandise or assistance. The carbon footprint is calculated from the total greenhouse gas emissions emitted by an organization, development, or result directly or indirectly. With this calculation, the impact on climate change can be quantified, and the possibilities of reducing both emissions and costs can be identified.

If you are thinking of a way to help the environment, changing the way you eat is one of the ways to do it.

Changing your diet can considerably reduce your carbon footprint since many studies have proven that a diet rich in animal meat is the most harmful to the environment. This type of diet is associated with the increased production of greenhouse gases.

I'll end a recent wave of controversy over whether eating meat is more sustainable than being vegan or vegan. A vegan menu is simply the most crucial way to reduce your influence on Earth, and

I will tell you why.

Going vegan or vegan reduces an individual's carbon footprint by 73%. Suppose the world stopped eating meat and dairy. In that case, global agricultural land use could be decreased by 75%, similar to the United States, China, Australia, and the EU combined.

The 'eat local food' argument for reducing your carbon footprint has emerged as one of the most popular lately. Even the United Nations normally recommends "eating local food" to decrease our environmental impact. But while this may intuitively make sense, it is a bit of a misnomer. This is because most of the emissions from food products do not come from their transport.

The only exception to this argument is food transported by air. However, this practice is not as common as is commonly believed. A very little percentage of the food we eat is transported by air; The food that most people assume comes by air comes by ship. But the few products that are transported by plane have a very large carbon footprint: they can emit up to 50 times more CO_2 than food transported by boat.

For most foods, particularly those that have the greatest impact on the environment, most of their greenhouse gas emissions result from land-use change. This refers to how lands in their natural state are transformed for human use and processes within the farm.

Many people had been convinced to go vegan after learning that the livestock industry generates more greenhouse gas emissions measured in CO2 equivalent (18 percent) than transport, according to the groundbreaking 2006 report published by the Organization of the United Nations for Food and Agriculture.

The report indicated that 14.5% of all human-produced greenhouse gases are associated with livestock, including 37% of all methane (twenty-three times more heat-trapping than CO2); Using 30% of the entire land area of the Earth, livestock is one of the main drivers of deforestation, especially in Latin America, where, for example, around 70% of the ancient forests of the Amazon have been turned into pasture.

Table 1. Average CO2 emissions.

Products	Consumpti on in kg per person per year	Carbon footprint per person per year
Poultry	28.63	30.75
Pork	48.92	173.15
Sheep and goat	2.16	75.64
meat beef	12.5	374.92
Wheat and by-products	93.88	17.90
Rice	8.32	10.65
Soy	0.02	0.01

Source: The carbon footprint and poultry production of José A. Castelló.

Later, in 2016, "Elementa" seemed to challenge the above by concluding that the vegetarian diet produces the most calories per landmass, with the vegan diet in fifth place. This research has frequently supported claims that vegetarian and omnivorous diets may be more sustainable than a vegan diet, even though it only measured the Earth's carrying capacity (performance) and was only limited to the EE. UU.

However, the information provided by "Elementa" did not last long. In 2020, a much more comprehensive study published in the journal "Science" observed nearly 40,000 farms in 119 communities, covering 40 food goods that account for 90% of everything consumed. It looked at land use and greenhouse gas emissions, freshwater use, water pollution, and air pollution.

Lead author Joseph Poore gets to the conclusion that "A vegan diet is presumably the best way to reduce the consequences on Earth, not just greenhouse gases, but global acidification, eutrophication, field use and water use. It is greatly more effective than cutting back on your flights or buying an electrical vehicle. "

The study has been met with strong praise from scientists who were not involved in the research. The fact that it comprises so much data and that it has been rigorously reviewed for publication in an of the two most prestigious scientific journals in the world (along with nature) also gives it the authority that is lacking in the study of "Elementa."

Thus, adopting certain behavioral guidelines for feeding ourselves can make a big difference in the individual carbon footprint generated by each person, from saving water to reducing pollution and forest loss.

You'll be kind to the world.

The vegan diet helps the environment: it reduces greenhouse gases, preserves water, Earth and saves lives. At the other extreme, meat and dairy production outnumber oil companies regarding the planet's pollution. They emit billions of tons of gas d and greenhouse effect that make global warming. I tell you the five ways in which the vegan diet helps the environment.

Help reduce global warming.

According to the World Meteorological Organization, in the last six years, the temperature of the Earth has risen alarmingly. This climate crisis puts the oceans and rivers, various animal and plant species, and human health at risk.

Therefore, it is urgent to adopt habits that help optimize the use of natural resources, minimize waste and pollution, and allow ecosystems to be restored.

Commonly, recycling is associated as the main pillar to stop global warming. Separating waste, choosing reusable products, and compost at home are valuable practices that help but are not enough: stopping eating animal products is the path societies must take to take care of the environment.

Factory farming (meat and dairy products) contributes 60% of greenhouse gas emissions. It increases dead zones in the oceans and the degradation of rivers, lakes, and seas, as indicated by the GreenPeace report.

The effects of climate change are visible: floods and forest fires, endangered species, drought. All of these issues will continue to get worse if we continue to consume animals.

Likewise, animal agriculture puts our subsistence at risk: it uses 83% of farmland but provides us with only 18% of the calories we consume; the world's top five meat and dairy producers emit more greenhouse gases combined than the top three oil companies. Livestock farms are also breeding grounds for the appearance of infectious diseases of zoonotic origin, such as COVID-19.

- Greenhouse gas emissions in 35 of the largest beef, pork, poultry, and dairy producers reach dangerous levels.

- Overproduction of meat companies: unregulated growth + government subsidies.

- Zero transparency: 50% of the largest meat and dairy producers do not report their emissions.

- Expectations: By 2050, meat and dairy farms will account for 80% of emissions.

Only governments can limit their growth together with responsible consumers. That is, those of us who know that the vegan diet helps the environment. Global meat consumption per capita has to fall to 16 kg per person by 2050 to avoid climate hazards. Indeed, the vegan diet helps the environment a lot.

It favors the recovery of the Earth.

Our vegan diet helps the environment, even if it is imperfect. Plant-based diets require only 1/3 of the amount of land used by the predatory system.

Wildlands lost to cattle farming would be recovered. Wild habitats are critical to maintaining biodiversity. The vegan diet also helps the environment in this regard: it is respectful of the environment.

Livestock pollutes the water, erodes, and weakens the soil. This is partly because cattle ranching generally leads to deforestation, which clears large swaths of land of the many elements (such as trees) that provide nutrients and elasticity to make room for livestock to graze. Instead, cultivating the soil with plant diversity nurtures it and leads to long-term resilience.

Improves the management and access to drinking water

Water is a limited natural resource, and the increase in its demand is an increasingly worrying factor: the scientific community estimates that by 2050, the global demand for freshwater -which currently represents only 2.5% of all water resources - will grow by more than 40%. Experts predict that the scarcity of this precious liquid will provoke the outbreak of armed conflicts, the so-called "water wars."

The agricultural division is the main consumer of freshwater (it uses 70% of the world's freshwater sources), an activity closely linked to livestock because a third of the fertile land on the planet is used for crops to feed animals.

For a plant-based diet, you need 0.7 liters of water on average per kilocalorie. This includes a mix of grains, sugars, roots, legumes, fruits, vegetables, and nuts. If we switch to a diet of dairy products and eggs, the need for water rises to 1.7 liters per kilocalorie (milk, butter, cheese, and eggs). But in the meat and fish category, the water average shoots up to more than four liters per kilocalorie, taking into account meat, chicken, pork, and fish according to the average consumption in industrialized countries.

The result is that a meat diet requires 4,480 liters of water per day, while a vegetarian requires 2,830 liters, a reduction of 37%. But the water savings are even greater if, keeping the total calories constant, we substitute all products of animal origin for vegetables. Thus, a vegan diet reduces water consumption to 2,380 liters per day, 47% less when we do without meat completely. The comparison shows that the change from meat to vegetables has a greater impact than taking another step towards veganism. This is because the water footprint per unit of meat is substantially higher than that of dairy.

Hundreds of millions of persons on the globe lack access to safe water. Many people struggle with water shortages due to droughts and poor management of water sources. At the same time, livestock consumes more freshwater than almost any other sector and pollutes freshwater. Can you measure the impact?

How much do we spend to produce a hamburger?

Ingredients	Water footprint (liters)
Lettuce (30 gr.)	7
Tomato (75 gr.)	15
Meat (150 gr).	2,325
Cheese (1 slice)	90
Catsup (1 envelope)	7

Source: www.waterfootprint.org

FIGHT HUNGER IN THE WORLD

It seems that the solution to a dire near future lies in the whole world turning to veganism. The human population is on an upward spiral toward possible overpopulation. Currently, the number of people exceeds seven billion. It is expected that by the next 30 years, this number will exceed nine billion inhabitants. This increase in population means that the world will have to find ways to increase the production of resources. Specifically, food, water, and fertile land will undoubtedly be the most important resources to maintain and increase. Currently, approximately 850 million people are suffering from famine, and if this continues, this number will only increase. The big problem with a diet based on meat and its derivatives, as it is in most Western countries, is that it is an incredibly demanding practice at the level of natural resources. A huge amount of water, land, food, and energy is necessary to produce animal products to raise, transport, and feed livestock. That is why adopting a diet based on plant products would be up to 160 times more efficient in resource use and would represent a 40% increase in food production worldwide to help eradicate hunger in the areas most affected by this problem.

In general, the industrial production of meat and dairy, which currently uses 34% of the crops suitable for human consumption to feed the animals they use, does not efficiently satisfy human nutritional needs.

If the entire American population went vegan, there would be enough food for them and 390 million others. Several researchers have determined that if the land currently used to produce meat, dairy, and eggs were used to grow a combination equivalent to its nutritional intake of potatoes, peanuts, soybeans, and other edible plants, the total food available would increase by 120%.

Raising farm animals requires tons of crops and grains. What if those crops were for people? If humans stopped using land and edible crops to sustain exploited animals for food, it would be possible to end world famine. Animals would find their food by natural means. And we would have taken a huge step.

IT PROMOTES BIODIVERSITY AND RESPECT FOR NATURE.

For most people, eating meat is as normal as sleeping at night. What happens when they tell us that it is, in fact, not normal? That our teeth are not originally designed for chewing meat? That slaughtering animals for nourishment is a cruel activity?

Yes, animals deserve a decent life. They are intelligent and gentle creatures. They should not suffer from birth to death. But that's the life many of them have when they are born on factory farms. Some meat generators are changing their models to accommodate public outrage at factory farms, but most meat found in restaurants and grocery stores is produced in poor condition.

The history of humanity is linked to countless conflicts and wars and numerous technological, social, and ethical advances, including progressive improvements in coexistence with other animal species. For a long time, animals have been considered mere objects, without intellectual or sensitive capacities, even without feelings. Therefore, they were not granted any kind of right or moral recognition. Today, we take a look at the controversial concept of animal welfare.

The ethical reasons for becoming vegan are interesting. They question killing living beings to feed ourselves since we can survive on the food of plant origin. The detractors of this position argue that a diet low in animal protein prevents full health. For this reason, it is not suited for children and pregnant women. In addition, they declare that, since animal species lack consciousness and reasoning equivalent to that of humans, the fact of consuming their meat does not make us criminals. We are at a high rational and moral level.

While the latter is true, so is the massive meat business. The industry raises millions of cattle, pigs, chickens, and other edible species then slaughters and sells them. It is important to emphasize that most killings are anything but painless. The most careful are cold and fast, but animals generally experience pain and suffering before they die. They are often crammed with no water, food, air, or room to move. Fattening methods can be subhuman, as in the case of geese, which are supercharged so that their liver grows enormously and is transformed, after slaughter, into a gourmet dish called *foie gras*.

The case of plants is different because they do not feel the above. The prospect of growing them just to eat is cruel compared to something like that in humans. And it is that animals, like us, have a central nervous system and therefore feel fear, stress, and pain.

Let us recognize that when we eat meat, we are eating someone, not something.

Why remove animals from their natural existence for it? Or perhaps, would it be justified to do the same with a dog or a cat? Most people dislike the thought of eating a man's best friend and then remember that it is an animal, just like cows or pigs. And it should be noted that pigs are smarter than you think.

It's not just about animal abuse; wildlife is rapidly disappearing. 75% of the terrestrial ecosystems and 66% of the marine habitat suffer serious alterations by human actions. Extinction rates for plants and animals indicate that there are about 1 million natural species in danger. Protected biodiversity must be a fact. It is about respecting the ecosystems of our home and treasuring them.

IT'S AN ACT OF SELF-LOVE.

As a diet, being vegan is following eating habits that reject products of animal origin. In this transition, doubts may arise about how recommendable it is for health. The reality is that having a plant-based diet is an excellent life decision because it brings many benefits to your health.

Leave worries behind. Vegan diets are nutritionally adequate, with benefits in preventing disease, according to the American Dietetic Association. In this position, the ADA even suggests that this diet is healthy during pregnancy, infancy, infancy, childhood, adolescence, and for athletes.

Similarly, the Academy of Nutrition and Dietetics, which has more than 100,000 certified specialists, stated to support the nutritional validity of a vegan diet for all types of people, at any stage of life, stating that:

"It is the stand of the Academy of Nutrition and Dietetics that a well-planned vegetarian and even vegan diet is healthy and nutritionally adequate, and can provide health benefits for the prevention and treatment of certain diseases. This diet is appropriate for all stages in the life cycle, including pregnancy, lactation, infancy, childhood, adolescence and old age, also for athletes ".

So it's no surprise that many high-performance athletes and

celebrities are leaving meat, dairy, and eggs out of their diet. Eating a healthy plant-based diet is not only a guarantee of adequate nutrition; it also avoids great health risks. I can guarantee that your body will receive the following benefits from following a vegan diet.

NUTRITIONAL VALUE

Numerous investigations have informed that vegan foods, when understood correctly, tend to include more fiber, antioxidants, potassium, magnesium, and vitamins A, C, and E. Vegan diets are packed with essential nutrients. Still, in the absence of meat, we must ensure that we continue to consume all the correct amounts of protein in other ways.

Protein is made up of small amino acids, which help our metabolism and keep our muscles, skin, and organs healthy. Vegan choices include seeds, peanut butter, nuts, legumes, and grains.

Iron is another critical nutrient and plays a crucial role in producing red blood cells that help bring oxygen throughout the body. Good sources come from iron or include beans, broccoli, raisins, wheat, and tofu.

IMPROVED MOOD

Studies have reported that vegans may be more peaceful than their carnivorous counterparts. Vegans and vegetarians were more moderate scores on depression tests and mood outlines than carnivores.

There is a freshness component in most plant-based foods, especially when it happens to organic produce, so this will clear our minds and keep our spirits positive.

DISEASE PREVENTION

How? Due to the understanding that they hold less soaked fat, vegan diets have been proven to reduce heart illness risk. Data proves that vegetarians and vegans suffer more sporadic diseases caused by a Western diet (e.g., coronary heart disease, hypertension, obesity, type 2 diabetes, diet-related cancers, diverticulitis, constipation, and gallstones, among others). This can be attributed to a higher fiber intake, flavonoids, antioxidants, phytonutrients, and carotenoids.

Foodborne illnesses, parasites, bacteria, and chemical toxins are more usual in commercial meats, poultry, and seafood than plant foods (especially organic fruits and vegetables). Vegans also eat less processed foods as a law, which blocks sickness.

Hormones like estrogen can be responsible for causing breast cancer if the levels progress too overdone. A New York study found that animal lipids can boost estrogen levels. Vegans have significantly more moderate estrogen levels than non-vegans due to the lower fat content of their diet. In addition, they have likewise certain transporter molecules, called globulins that bind to sex hormones, that circulate in the blood and have the function of holding on to sex hormones, keeping them inactive until they are needed. Fatty foods do the opposite: they increase estrogen.

In addition to decreasing the risks of certain diseases, the vegan diet can further help decrease the onset of migraine strikes. Migraines are often linked to our diets, and food is a common trigger. Vegan diets, particularly organic ones, are much more transparent and less inclined to trigger migraine outbreaks. Foods like cheese and chocolate are also frequent culprits.

This is why vegans have been determined to enjoy longer and healthier lives related to those who hold meat in their diets.

WEIGHT LOSS

An account of following a vegan diet is the positive effect it has on our weight. To accomplish weight loss, it is important to consume fewer calories than normal. Vegetarian and vegan diets can support due to many factors.

Plant-based diets include many fruits, vegetables, whole grains, legumes, nuts, and seeds. These foods work to be high in fiber, a dietary ingredient that reduces hunger and increases feelings of fullness. Thanks to this, fewer calories will be used without even realizing it and without having to starve.

Due to its higher content of fruits and vegetables, a vegan diet (if you do not eat an abundance of processed products, particularly bakery and pastries) provides more negligible calories for the same volume of food.

We can say that 300 g of broccoli or 283 g of melon carries 100 calories to get an idea. However, foods with less or no fiber produce the same calories with much less volume: 56 g of chicken or 28 g of cheese also provide 100 calories. You fill up with more, with just 30 g of cheese or 300 g of broccoli. Further needs to be said.

Many of the foods located on omnivorous foods each day include animal products. These incorporate high-calorie, low-nutrient choices like processed foods and baked goods, making it simple to overindulge. As these products include ingredients or additives of animal origin, they are out of the vegan diet.

As a result, vegans usually weigh less and do not suffer from overweight bodies due to a diet constituted of fewer calories in the sort of grains, seeds, nuts, legumes, vegetables, and fruits. Vegans are also more informed of healthy foods and consequently tend to eat better. Plant foods also tend to be easier to digest, appearing in a better figure and the inadequacy of overweight.

IMPROVED ATHLETIC PERFORMANCE

While most effective people focus on protein intake, more and more competitors follow carbohydrate-rich, high-fat, and vitamin-mineral-rich vegan or vegetarian nutrition for optimal muscular performance. World tennis stars such as The Venus sisters and Serena Williams have been vegan since 2011.

A careful diet within the vegan diet can lead an athlete to become an athlete with an equal caloric and nutritious diet quality or better than a person who is not.

One of the great myths that carry veganism is that the protein ingested is not enough, which is false. Quinoa, soy, or amaranth have all the necessary amino acids that our body needs. Soy supplies more protein than meat (100g of soy would provide us with 36g of protein while 100g of beef only 20g). The rest of the protein does not have all the essential amino acids. It is possible to obtain it by combining it, such as combining legumes with nuts or legumes with cereals.

Carbohydrates are responsible for keeping muscles firm. Suppose enough carbohydrates are provided in the diet. In that case, the muscle will be packed with glycogen and will be able to perform better during workouts. Carbohydrates are the principal intake of energy for the body. To gain and maintain size, they should account for most of the caloric intake of an athlete's training strength. Complex carbohydrates such as oatmeal, legumes, broccoli, spinach, tomatoes, berries, and soy are very helpful; they keep your blood sugar level stable, giving you more energy and helping to promote muscle growth.

YOU WON'T GIVE UP AMAZING FLAVORS.

Vegan diets are the choice of more and more people around the world. Although it may seem surprising, the habit of eating dishes similar to meat and fish, in reality, they are not, is more widespread.

Gastronomic advances and the discovery of new ways to simulate the taste of meat allow more people to eat foods that can substitute for meat but have the advantage of not being of animal origin.

There is a growing variety of substitute products suitable for vegan diets, called meats for vegans or vegetarians. Below I highlight the most prominent foods of this type.

Seitan

Seitan is one of the greatest meat substitutes in the world. It is a food of oriental origin, specifically Chinese, whose consumption has spread throughout the world.

So many vegans choose this meat substitute because it is a food whose physical properties are very similar to real meat. Seitan has a brown or dark appearance and an uneven texture that could fool many. It can be cooked in all the ways that a piece of beef, chicken, or pork is cooked: grilled, battered or breaded, fried or stewed.

One of the favorite nourishment of vegans and a highly

demanded product, seitan is made mainly from wheat gluten and soy sauce. In addition to being a cruelty-free food, it contains many nutrients, among which proteins, vitamins, and different types of minerals stand out.

Tofu

Tofu is a food of Chinese stock made from soybeans, water, and coagulant. It is a common dish in Asian food in general and in Japanese and Chinese in particular. However, the boom in the influence of oriental cuisine has caused the consumption of tofu to expand throughout the world. In addition to being a highly appreciated food in Asian cuisine, tofu has been used for many years as a substitute food for meat for vegans or vegetarians. Although raw, it does not have much flavor. You can add a lot of sauces and spices to make it more delicious.

Tofu is obtained from the coagulation of soy milk. The preparation consists of coagulating the milk to separate the liquid from the solid part, creating a curd that will be pressed to give it the desired shape, in a process similar to that of obtaining cheese from milk.

Tempeh

Tempeh is also a meat substitute food widely consumed by vegans or vegetarians. It is a food of Indonesian origin made in a similar way to tofu.

Tempeh is obtained from the cooking and fermentation of yellow soybeans, giving it an appearance and texture alike to that of certain meats.

Like seitan, tempeh can be cooked in many ways and is a food that requires very light digestion due to its minimal level of fat.

Soy

Soy is a plant widely used in vegan and vegetarian diets. It is a versatile food since it can be used to prepare meat-like foods, especially using textured soy; this includes tofu and tempeh, which we discussed earlier.

Vegan burgers, vegan steaks, and all kinds of meat-like foods are made from soybeans. The great contribution of proteins and carbohydrates of soybeans and its low-fat content make it a very suitable food for vegans and vegetarians.

Lentils

Lentils are also a central food for vegans. In recent years has become a widely used ingredient to make meat for vegans and vegetarians.

Its great nutritional contribution makes it a necessary food for people who do not consume.

BEST DELICIOUS VEGAN MEAT

VEGAN PORK RECIPES

Pork is one of the most commonly cooked meats on the planet and we've chosen to place our twist into these insignificant yet brilliant pork plans that will make them anticipate each tidbit.

1. Daikon Bacon

Daikon Vegans don't have to bid farewell to the persuading taste regarding bacon ceaselessly, not with our Vegan Bacon Recipe! In this situation, we make a veggiedarling-friendly variety of the remarkable breakfast food, bacon! Our phony on bacon is so like real bacon that you will not see the capability. With our amazing formula, your veggie darling's inside and out-organized rendition will have the outstandingly firm surface and a sharp taste that bacon is known for.

While bacon is a pleasant wellspring of omega-3 unsaturated fats, it likewise has high extents of soaked fat. An extreme proportion of ingested fat outcomes raised cholesterol, which is terrible for your heart. Notwithstanding, secretly acquired plant-based bacon may not be better by a comparative token. Like traditional bacon, they're likewise dealt with, so it's cleverer to eat with some limit. The accommodating thing our hand-created formula utilizes is daikon radish. This plant is high in supplement C, phosphorus, and potassium. Daikon Bacon is quite one of the most unprecedented plant-based bacon out there! They approach the taste and look of run-of-the-mill bacon.

Cook unobtrusive cuts of the smoky, firm, and sharp bacon the veggie darling way, utilizing Daikon radish. You will not see the separation among bonafide and veggie darlings with our Vegan Bacon Recipe!

Organizing: 35 mins

Cooking: 25 mins

Full scale: 1 hr

INGREDIENTS

For Vegan Bacon:

- 10 oz new radish ideally Daikon

- salt to taste

- cooking shower

For Marinade:

- 2 tsp smoked paprika

- 1 tsp soy sauce

- 2 tbsp coconut oil

- ½ tsp salt

- 2 tsp garlic powder

- 1 tbsp maple syrup

INSTRUCTIONS

Vegetarian Bacon:

1. Preheat the broiler to 325 degrees F.

2. Make long, meager strips out of radish by stripping daintily utilizing a peeler.

3. Layer the radish strips on a heating plate fixed with paper towels. Sprinkle the radish strips with salt, then, at that point, cover with another paper towel.

4. Set to the side for around 15 minutes.

Marinade:

1. In a bowl, consolidate the paprika, soy sauce, coconut oil, salt, garlic powder, and maple syrup, and race until equally joined.

2. Remove the paper towel on top of the radish and wipe off any overabundance of salt and dampness.

3. Transfer the stripped radish into the marinade and blend until very much covered.

4. Marinate for something like 15 minutes.

5. After marinating, channel radish marginally.

6. Spritz the cooking shower on a heating plate to keep the radish from staying.

7. Neatly mastermind the radish strips onto the lubed heating plate.

8. Roast them on the stove for around 25 minutes, or until brilliant brown.

9. Serve alongside veggie lover eggs, hash brown, and your favored ketchup or dressing. Appreciate!

2. Thick-cut seitan bacon

This is exceptionally delicious. It's additionally modest to make yet takes a small while so it merits bending over the amounts to make an enormous group – it freezes for as long as 90 days so put it all on the line. It is easy yet it's a cycle fifty so get out every one of the fixings and hardware first – it will smooth out the activity pleasantly!

Yet, what is seitan in any case,

Seitan – or gluten – is the first meat elective. This delicious dish begins in China in the sixth century and was frequently eaten by veggie lover Buddhist priests, among others. It has since permeated around the Far East, eg Japan, and Vietnam, and is utilized in contemporary Western veggie and vegetarian food.

It is made by washing wheat flour batter with water until all the starch granules have been eliminated. Purchasing indispensable gluten flour implies the work has been accomplished for you! High in protein, low in fat, and thick in surface, it fits a wide range of dishes, including sautés, 'steaks', rashers, shop cuts for sandwiches, meatballs/pieces and that's just the beginning.

While it is a superb wellspring of protein, it is unadulterated gluten so best not eaten more than one time per week – it's in every case great to incorporate as wide an assortment of food sources as could be expected, eg beats, tofu, nuts, whole grains, vegetables, products of the soil like. Seitan is inadmissible for the gluten or wheat bigoted.

Fixings

This formula utilizes some specialty fixings yet these are working their direction steadily into the standard…

- Vital gluten flour
- Liquid smoke

- Nutritional yeast chips

- Red miso glue

RED DOUGH

Dry:

- 1 Cup Vital Wheat Gluten

- 1/4 Cup soy flour (or garbanzo flour)

- 2 Tablespoons Nutritional Yeast

- 2 teaspoons ordinary paprika

- 2 teaspoons smoked paprika

- 1 teaspoon garlic powder

- 1 teaspoon onion powder

- 1/2 teaspoon dark pepper

Wet:

- 2/3 Cup warm water

- 3 Tablespoons Tamari

- 3 Tablespoons maple syrup

- 2 Tablespoons tomato glue

- 1 teaspoon Liquid Smoke

- 2 Tablespoons nut oil

WHITE DOUGH

Dry:

- 1/2 Cup Vital Wheat Gluten

- 2 Tablespoons garbanzo flour (or soy flour)

- 1 Tablespoon Nutritional Yeast

- 1/2 teaspoon garlic powder

- 1 teaspoon onion powder

- 1/2 teaspoon fine ocean salt

Wet:

- 1/2 Cup warm water

- 1 Tablespoon nut oil

Directions

1. Red Dough: In a medium blending bowl, dry whisk together the dry fixings. Independently consolidate every one of the wet fixings and mix or rush until very much mixed. Add wet fixings to dry fixings and mix with a spoon until blended. Shape red batter into a fat log and cut it into three equivalent pieces.

2. White Dough: In a little blending bowl, dry whisk together the dry fixings. To the dry fixings, include the water and oil, and mix with a spoon until blended.

3.   Divide the white batter into two equivalent pieces.

4.   Lay a piece of cling wrap on the counter and put one piece of the red mixture on it.

5.   Cover the red batter with one more piece of saran wrap.

6.   Gently carry out the mixture until it's around 1/4-inch tall. I propose making it approx. 6″ x 7. Spray a piece of tin foil with a cooking shower and move the straightened batter onto it. I did this by getting the piece of plastic and flipping it onto the foil.

Rehash the moving system, substituting the white and red mixtures, and stacking them onto the primary piece that you laid onto the foil. Try not to attempt to make them great.

8.   Place a piece of cling wrap on top of the stacked battery.

9.   Rest a medium-substantial book on top of the plastic for around 20 minutes.

10.   Remove the cling wrap, and enclose the entire chunk of bacon with tin foil.

On a heating sheet, prepare at 300 degrees for 45 minutes.

11.   Your seitan will be a piece half-cooked, however, this is acceptable because it will be simpler to cut, and it will sear better.

12.   Cool and cut.

13. When you're prepared to utilize the bacon: sauté in a non-leave skillet with a touch of veggie lover margarine and a couple of sprinkles of preparing salt.

3.Bacon from mochi (sweet rice flour)

When you combine rice and seaweed, mochi is low in saturated fat and very low in cholesterol. It is also a good source of Vitamins A, C, E (Alpha Tocopherol), and K, Niacin, Pantothenic Acid, and Phosphorus. It's also a very good source of Riboflavin, Folate, Calcium, Iron, Magnesium, Copper, and Manganese.

INGREDIENTS

- 1 cup short- or medium-grain Japanese rice

- 2 tablespoon potato starch

- 1 package of nori (seaweed)

- ¼ cup soy sauce

- ¼ cup pickled ginger

INSTRUCTIONS

- Cook one cup of rice in a rice cooker or boil on the stove.

- Let cool for five minutes

- Knead with a blender until smooth.

- Sprinkle with potato starch and flatten.

- Cut into squares, wrap in plastic, keep in the fridge.

- When you want to prepare a mochi snack, put a square in a warm toaster oven at 325°F (163°C) for 5 to 10 minutes. They will puff up.

- Wrap in nori and dip in soy sauce. Add pickled ginger for some sweetness.

4. Smoked watermelon ham

The smoked watermelon is by and large what it says it is. Charged as a veggie lover option in contrast to a Thanksgiving broil, it is intended to seem as though a ham, directly down to the singed coat and delicate, substantial surface.

A sweet and pungent dish, this smoked watermelon ham might

look a great deal like its pork partner yet you can be guaranteed this formula is without meat.

Preparation:30 minutes

Cooking:3 hours

Total:3 hours 30 minutes

Fixings

For the Smoke Watermelon:

- 1large watermelon, seedless

- ½cupkosher salt

- 3tbspcoconut sugar

- 1tbspchili powder

- 1tbspsmoked paprika

- 1½tspfreshly ground dark pepper

- 2tspgarlic powder

- 2tsponion powder

- ½tspground cloves

- 3cupshickory chips, soaked in cool water for 60 minutes

- orange, or new rosemary or thyme twigs, for decorating

For the Chipotle and Honey Glaze:

- 2 tsp canola oil

- 2 tsp garlic, minced

- 2 tsp fresh ginger, piece of new ginger, stripped, minced

- ½ cup coconut sugar

- ½ cup raw agave

- ½ cup fresh squeezed orange

- 2tsp dijon mustard

- 1 tbsp pureed chipotle in adobo

- 1 tsp kosher salt

- ½ tsp worcestershire sauce

Guidelines

1. Brine and smoke the watermelon: Carefully cut the closures off of the watermelon. Turn the watermelon onto a level side, then, at that point, remove the skin, working cautiously to cut off as little tissue as could be expected.

2. Discard the skin.

3. Lay the watermelon on the cutting board the long way. Track down the side of the watermelon that has the biggest surface region and set that face-up.

4. On the highest point of the watermelon, cut 1-inch corner to corner cuts in inverse ways to shape a cross-bring forth design.

5. In a medium bowl, whisk together the salt, coconut sugar, stew powder, paprika, pepper, garlic powder, onion powder, and cloves.

6. Rub the flavor combination all around the watermelon, making a point to get some between the cross-incubate cuts, yet being mindful so as not to tear the watermelon.

7. Set a wire rack inside a rimmed heating sheet. Spot the watermelon on the rack, cross-bring forth side up, and refrigerate, uncovered, for something like 12 hours.

8. Preheat broiler to 450 degrees F.

9. Drain everything except 2 tablespoons of the hickory chip dousing fluid, then, at that point, spread the chips and saved fluid in an even layer over the lower part of a simmering container. Set a simmering rack on top.

10. Place the watermelon, cross-bring forth side up on the broiling rack. Cover the skillet firmly with hardcore foil.

11. Bake the watermelon for 30 minutes.

12. Reduce the stove temperature to 250 degrees F. Keep preparing the watermelon for 3 hours then, at that point, eliminate the foil and meal an additional 3 hours.

13. While the watermelon cooks, make the chipotle and nectar coat: Heat the canola oil in a huge skillet over medium-high hotness.

14. Once the oil is gleaming, add the garlic and ginger and cook, blending habitually, for 1 to 2 minutes or until light brilliant brown in shading and exceptionally fragrant.

15. Add the coconut sugar, nectar, squeezed orange, mustard, chipotle, salt, and Worcestershire sauce and cook, mixing continually until the blend is equitably consolidated.

16. Bring to a stew and afterward decrease the hotness to medium. Cook, mixing regularly, for 10 to 12 minutes more or until diminished considerably.

17. After 6 hours, eliminate the watermelon from the stove and turn the oven on high.

18. Carefully eliminate the rack from the broiling skillet and spot it on a heating sheet. Dispose of the abundance of fluid and hickory chips from the container. Return the rack with the watermelon to the cooking container.

19. Brush ¼ cup of the coating over the highest point of the watermelon. Sear for 10 to 12 minutes, pivoting the container on a case-by-case basis until the coating has uniformly caramelized.

20. Using long metal spatulas to help the watermelon, move it to a huge serving platter with cut oranges or new rosemary or thyme twigs.

21. Glaze the warm watermelon with another ¼ cup of the

coating. Cut the watermelon and present it with the excess coating close by.

22.   Enjoy!

5. Grill Mushroom ribs

What's the neatest thing you'll have the option to blend your wonderful ribs in with? a decent barbecue sauce. Its sweet, smoky person goes perfectly with the meat, and each one you wish to attempt to now could be choose an improbable aspect to go with it. We've attempted a blend of mushrooms and celery, one thing lightweight that changes the heavier ribs.

Fixings

- 1-pound pork ribs.
- 1 teaspoon vegetable oil.
- 1 teaspoon paprika powder.
- salt.
- 8 mushrooms.
- 4 celery stems, pieces.
- 2 tablespoons of barbecue sauce.

Directions

1. heat up the oven to 400 degrees F/200 degrees C.

2. Spot the ribs on your working surface.

3. Shower some vegetable oil over them. Season them with salt and paprika.

4. Spot the mushrooms and celery stems on an elongated preparing plate.

5. Spot the ribs on high of the veggies. unfurl the barbecue sauce over them.

6. Prepare the ribs for the ensuing hour.

6. Vegan Pork Rinds (Fried Rice Paper)

Plant-based bite organization Outstanding Foods has given Pig-out Pigless Pork Rinds, that square measure an eater choice in distinction to customary singed pig skins. The skins square measure loaded with super molecule, ready till lightweight and recent, and ready to create an existent pork style, as indicated by the organization.

veggie lover pork skins created victimization singed rice paper! This bite is amusing to create and that they cook like enchantment in less than seconds! they are super crisp and have the same surface as pork skins, with no creature fixings! Have some sensible times getting ready them any means that you simply want. This bite will not ever get exhausting! you'll be able to even prepare the singed paper with untidy wholesome yeast and create camp-made eater cheese puffs.

As a feeder, nothing seems to be less attention-grabbing to Pine Tree State than pork skins, however, this cooked paper is tasty and therefore the surface is astounding. ready with some salt and smoke-cured paprika these crisps area unit addictive. just in case you were a private that appreciated pork skins before surrendering meat, you may treasure these!

This formula is;

- fast and straightforward to make!

- a veggie-lover, sans soy, and protein bite that everyone can treasure.

- tender and delectable!

INGREDIENTS

1. paper - These area units the extent sheets that you simply unremarkably absorb water and create into summer rolls. I attempted it with varied brands and that they all worked one thing terribly similar.

2. Oil - for profound preparation. Any unbiased increased oil can work.

3. smoke-cured Paprika - to allow them a smoky character.

4. Umami Mushroom Seasoning - (discretionary) if you have got this, it offers it to a larger extent a considerable character, nonetheless you'll exclude it.

5. Salt - for a few characters.

6. Cayenne Pepper - merely a scramble for a fiery feeder pork skin

48

flavor. (discretionary)

7. different facultative Seasonings - My family likewise enjoys Tony Chachere's creole seasoning, previous Bay seasoning, or maybe some nutrient yeast. plow ahead and obtain originative with however you season them.

Accommodating instruments

- Deep pullet - it's helpful, nonetheless you'll likewise effectively utilize a huge pot with around a 1/2 in. of oil.

- device - to require the rotisserie paper out of the new oil.

INSTRUCTIONS

- Cut a pair of bits of dry paper into very little items. (You will create them in any form that you simply want like triangles or strips.)

- Heat oil during a profound pullet or a pot to around 350 F. (If you do not have a measuring device, give a touch take a look at piece of paper. It ought to sizzle and self-praise at once.combine the seasoning and prepare it to sprinkle on the singed paper. Spot a towel on a plate to retain copious oil.

- supply a few of bits of paper at a time into the new oil. Following a few of moments, it'll self-praise and quit sizzling, currently eliminate it with utensils. (Shake the singed items over the pot of oil. The knocks on the singed paper can generally snare the oil.)

- forthwith sprinkle them along with your ideal seasoning mix.

Genius tips

1. Kitchen scissors stir extraordinary for cutting up the paper into the best form.

2. You will notice that the oil is hot enough after you place a bit of paper in it and it and puffs up and bubbles during a flash. If the paper stays delicate for a few of moments once you set it within the oil, then, at that time, it is not hot enough.

3. Fry the paper till it equal sizzling, then, at that time, take away it from the new oil with utensils. use caution, the knocks entice a little of the oil and it'll flee as you are taking them out.

4. Is it correct to mention that they're while not gluten?

5. Indeed, merely certify to envision the fixings on your paper bundle. a couple of brands do add some flour, therefore twofold check little doubt.

Capacity

Vegetarian pork skins area unit best devoured new, nonetheless you'll keep them during a water/airproof sack at temperature for as long as five days. just in case it's damp, they're going to get lifeless, however, you'll place them on a treat sheet and prepare them at 200°

F (93° C) for around five minutes to dry them out and create them recent another time.

7. Vegetarian force Pork Sandwich (BBQ Soy Curls)

This feeder force pork sandwich is washed in my refined while not sugar grill sauce and finished off with a customized veggie-lover coleslaw! It makes the best feeder sandwich for your next grill or cookout! while not protein, sans dairy, and overflowing with flavor, everyone can partake during this protein-pressed sandwich!

I see immense different plans out there for force jackfruit sandwiches and that they area unit acceptable, nonetheless, bound people merely do not look after the surface or style of jackfruit. This force pork sandwich created with soy twists is loaded with macromolecule and is genuinely a filling and fulfilling supper!

Prep Time:10 mins

Cook Time:10 mins Complete Time:20 mins around 5 minutes to prepare.

What area unit Soy Curls?

Soy Curls area unit got dried out soy macromolecule created by pantryman Foods. At the purpose once re-hydrated, they absorb the sort of the stock and alter into a considerable surface. At the purpose after you modification the sort of the stock, you alter the sort of soy twist too.

Make it style like force pork

To make soy twists style like pork, you just ought to re-hydrate soy twists during a stock that features a pork-like character and with flavors that people would unremarkably placed on pork. To do this, I add Bragg's Liquid Aminos, Dijon mustard, and a couple of flavors to effervescent water to form a stock and later on re-hydrated the soy twists in it. once they absorb this character, essentially sauté them with Associate in Nursing onion and coat everything with grill sauce.

INGREDIENTS

For the "pulled pork" increased stock

- Braggs Liquid Aminos - or tamari or soy (soy sauce is not sans gluten). i like the flavour of the Bragg's, however, all have a comparative style.

- Dijon Mustard - this can be essential to allow it a force pork flavor.

   Boiling Water - this can be the fluid base of your "pork" stock.

- Garlic Powder - for a few characters.

- Black Pepper - new ground is heavenly if you have got it.

INGREDIENTS

For the stock to re-hydrate the soy twists:

- one cup effervescent water

- a pair of tbsp Bragg's fluid Aminos or Tamari or soy

- one tbsp entire grain Dijon mustard

- 1/2 tsp new ground pepper

- 1/4 tsp garlic powder

For cooking the soy twists:

- three cups pantry man soy twists

- 1 tbsp oil for browning onion

- 1 little onion diced

- 1/4 tsp salt

- 1 1/2 cup grill sauce

- vegan coleslaw (discretionary)

- 8 rolls or buns to collect the sandwich

For the sandwich

- Soy twists - this is your vegetarian "meat." This is my number one supper choice to utilize. You can likewise utilize jackfruit, mushrooms, or some other meat substitute that you need, simply overlook the water since there will be no requirement for rehydrating. (You will in any case need the flavoring to season your meat substitute).

- Onion - for some zing. (discretionary, yet suggested).

- Oil - to sauté the onion and soy twists.

Salt - for some characters.

- Barbecue Sauce - you can utilize most locally acquired brands or utilize my formula for refined sans sugar grill sauce.

- Coleslaw - to layer in your sandwich for that bona fide pulled pork sandwich taste.

- Rolls or Sandwich Buns - Any vegetarian assortment will work. On the off chance that you need it to be without gluten, I have discovered that Schar brand rolls function admirably.

INSTRUCTIONS

1. Make some veggie lover coleslaw whenever wanted and put it away.

2. Combine every one of the elements for the stock in an enormous bowl and give it a mix.

3. Quickly add the soy twists and let them absorb the kinds of the stock. Mix incidentally to ensure all the soy twists get re-hydrated in the stock.

4. Saute a diced onion in 1 tbsp of oil in a huge griddle on low while the soy twists are dousing.

5. Sprinkle the onion with salt and cook for around 5 minutes until they are clear.

6. Add the re-hydrated soy twists to the griddle and turn up the

warmth to medium and saute for around 5 additional minutes.

7. Pour the grill sauce over the soy twists and coat well.

8. Assemble the pulled pork sandwiches by putting the cooked soy twists on a bun finished off with vegetarian coleslaw.

Expert tips

- You can utilize any mustard. I like the kind of mustard with entire mustard seeds. You could likewise add 1/2 tsp of entire mustard seed alongside the mustard as well.

- You can discard the onions whenever wanted, yet at the same time, cook the soy twists for around 5 minutes to help the flavors mix.

- If the soy twists are still somewhat hard after dousing, add a modest quantity of heated water until they are re-hydrated totally.

  If there is still some stock at the lower part of the bowl, add it to the griddle with the soy twists.

Picking your sauce

Most grill sauces that they sell at the store are vegetarian, so you are presumably protected utilizing your #1 sauce. However, these sauces do contain a huge load of sugar. I needed a vegetarian grill sauce that wasn't predominantly sweet and didn't utilize refined sugar, so I concocted my own, veggie lover BBQ sauce, improved distinctly with maple syrup. Indeed, even my children incline toward my handcrafted sauce to the locally acquired adaptations and it just takes a Vegan Pulled Pork Sandwich

INSTRUCTIONS

1. some veggie lover coleslaw whenever wanted and put it away.

2. In a huge bowl join every one of the elements for the stock and mix.

3. Quickly add the soy twists and let them absorb the kinds of the stock. Mix every so often to ensure all the soy twists get re-hydrated in the stock.

4. Make While the soy twists are drenching, saute a diced onion in 1 tbsp of oil in an enormous griddle on low.

5. Sprinkle the onion with salt and cook for around 5 minutes until they are clear.

6. Add the re-hydrated soy twists to the griddle and turn up the warmth to medium and saute for around 5 additional minutes.

7. Pour the grill sauce of decision over the soy twists and coat well.

8. Assemble the pulled pork sandwiches by putting the cooked soy twists on a bun finished off with veggie lover coleslaw.

Formula Notes

- You can utilize any mustard. I like the kind of mustard with entire mustard seeds. You could likewise add 1/2 tsp of entire mustard seed alongside the mustard as well.

- You can discard the onions whenever wanted, yet, cook the soy twists for around 5 minutes to help the flavors mix.

- If the soy twists are still somewhat hard after splashing, add a limited quantity of heated water until they are re-hydrated totally.

- If there is still some stock at the lower part of the bowl, add it to the griddle with the soy twists.

8. Vegan Pepperoni

This vegetarian pepperoni formula will just astound you! Fiery, delightful, substantial pepperoni produced using wheat gluten and flavored flawlessly! Make vegetarian pepperoni pizza, pepperoni rolls, calzones, or go through it to zest your veggie lover charcuterie board. This seitan pepperoni prepares in minutes and adds a substantial zesty kick to any dinner.

High protein vegetarian meats produced using cooked wheat gluten are known as seitan, and this

pepperoni seitan is one amongst the smallest amount exacting of all. after you understand however simple this sausage is to create, you may create it over and over. Dice it up and prepare it into feeder salad, green groceries lover bolognese sauce, or maybe place it in green groceries lover lasagna, feeder heated pasta, or stuffed shells for a tasty meat substitute.

INGREDIENTS

- Oil - for a chic character. I prefer refined copra oil, however, any nonpartisan increased oil can work. you'll be able to exclude it assumptive you would like it to be while not oil.

  smoke-dried Paprika - you'll be able to likewise utilize customary paprika additionally to 1/2 tsp of fluid smoke.

- Red Pepper Flakes - you'll be able to amendment the total to manage the degree of flavor.

- recent Ground Black Pepper - utilize new ground for the most effective character. you'll be able to trade it out for standard dark pepper, however, it'll not be terribly as tasty.

- Onion Powder-for some zing.

- Garlic Powder - for a few zing.

- Fennel Seeds - for a standard character. Exclude on the off probability that you just do not take care of the character.

- Whole Mustard Seeds - discretionary for a few character. act and ditch them, however, i prefer the character and surface that they add.

- Water - or low atomic number 11 vegetable stock

- Salt - on the off probability that you just would favor to not utilize salt, you'll be able to trade it out with one tablespoon of Bragg's Liquid Aminos or soy.

- catsup - for flavor and slight pleasantness. you'll be able to likewise utilize tomato glue and a touch sugar.

- important protein|gluten} - this can be a high-protein gluten flour. you ought to utilize gluten and no alternative reasonably flour to induce the sausage to figure with this strategy. there's no sans protein trade for this. you'll be able to assume that it's all things thought of vital supermarkets

INGREDIENTS

- one tablespoon refined copra oil or any unbiased increased oil

- two teaspoons smoke-dried paprika

- 1/2 teaspoon red pepper chips

- 1/2 teaspoon new ground dark pepper

- 1/2 teaspoon fennel seeds

- 1/2 teaspoon entire mustard seeds discretionary

- 1/2 teaspoon onion powder

- 1/2 teaspoon garlic powder

- 1/3 cup water

- one teaspoon salt

- one tablespoon catsup

- seven tablespoons imperative gluten

Prep Time:10 minutes

Cook Time:35 minutes

INSTRUCTIONS

1. In an exceedingly very little pan, heat the oil over low heat and add the smokedried paprika, red pepper chips, dark pepper, fennel seeds, mustard seeds, garlic powder, and onion powder.

2. Stir the flavors around within the heat oil and let the flavors sprout for around three minutes, then, at that time, eliminate from heat. (Make absolute to simply heat the oil and not consume the flavors.)

3. Add cold water, ketchup, and salt and blend well.

4. combine in five tbsp of the indispensable gluten with a element spatula, then, at that time, ply within the excess two tablespoons of gluten along with your hand.

5. form the sausage into a log form and wrap it firmly in foil. (You will enclose it with a layer of fabric before intromission it by foil on the off probability that you just do not want the foil to contact your food.)

6. Place the sausage into a liner bin and steam for forty minutes.

7. permit it to cool down and after cut and use as you'd sausage.

MORE rationalization ON directions

- In an exceedingly very little pan, heat one tbsp oil over low heat and add two tsp smoke-dried paprika, 1/2 tsp red pepper drops, 1/2 tsp dark pepper, 1/2 tsp fennel seeds, 1/2 tsp mustard seeds, 1/2 tsp garlic powder, and 1/2 tsp onion powder.

- Stir the flavors around within the heat oil and let the flavors sprout for around three minutes, then, at that time, eliminate from heat. (Make absolute to simply heat the oil and not consume the flavors.)

- Add 1/3 cup cold water, one tbsp catsup, and one tsp salt and blend well.

- combine in five tablespoons of the imperative gluten with a element spatula, then, at that time, massage within the leftover two tablespoons of gluten along with your hand.

- form the sausage into a log form and wrap it firmly in foil. (You will enclose it with a layer of fabric before close it by foil if you do not want the foil to contact your food.)

- Place the sausage into a liner instrumentality and steam for forty minutes.

- permit it to cool down and after cut and use as you'd sausage.

Formula Notes

- important gluten is an especially fine powder and it gets untidy quickly. whereas adding the flour, hold the estimating cup low within the bowl thus you do not have a haze of powder.

- Feel allowed to vary the flavors as you'd like.

- scale back the red pepper for fewer hot sausage.

- Add a scramble of cayenne for very fiery sausage.

- If you do not have a liner bushel, you'll be able to utilize a modest amount of water and block instrumentality rings at the lower a part of your pot to carry the sausage out of the water. merely check and extra service the water on a independent basis.

- Wash your bowl and utensils in very plight. this can "cook" the protein and stop it from being tacky.

62

Master Tips

Vital wheat gluten is an exceptionally fine powder and it gets untidy quickly. While adding the flour, hold the estimating cup low in the bowl so you don't have a haze of powder.

- Feel allowed to change the flavors as you would prefer.

- Reduce the red pepper for less zesty pepperoni.

- Add a scramble of cayenne for especially zesty pepperoni.

- If you don't have a liner crate, you can utilize a modest quantity of water and spot jam container rings at the lower part of your pot to lift the pepperoni out of the water. Simply check and top off the water on a case-by-case basis.

- Wash your bowl and utensils in extremely hot water. This will "cook" the gluten and prevent it from being tacky.

Surface

- Small changes in the measure of indispensable wheat gluten you use will change the surface of the end-product. More gluten gives you a firmer surface and less gives you a milder surface.

- I track down the best surface is accomplished if you add fundamental wheat gluten until the batter doesn't handily ingest more, yet less than the mixture becomes rubbery and you can't frame it into a smooth shape.

- You may likewise decide to discard the oil and just add the flavors to the water. This delivers an exceptionally firm and chewy pepperoni, but on the other hand, it's inadequate about the mouthfeel that fat gives. I tried it the two different ways commonly and my family couldn't choose which one they loved better. I urge you to mess with it until you get the consistency that you want.

- Note: Your pepperoni will keep on firming up once it cools totally.

9. Sweet and Sour Pork Recipe

A most loved takeout Chinese dish, this prepared pork formula is made with battered pork threw in a sweet and tart sauce then, at that point, singed to a firm completion.

Preparation:15 minutes

Cooking:20 minutes

Total:35 minutes

INGREDIENTS

For the Sweet and Sour Sauce:

- ½cuphoney

- 6tbsprice vinegar

- 4tsp soy sauce

- 3tbsptomato glue

- 1tbspcornstarch

- 2tbspwater

For the Pork:

- 1½lbspork tenderloin
- 1tsp Kosher salt, divided
- ½tsp black pepper, divided
- ¾cupall-reason flour
- ⅓cup corn starch
- 2eggs, large
- 2cups vegetable oil
- 1tbsp garlic, minced
- 1cup white onions
- 1cupred chime pepper
- 1cup green chime pepper
- 1cup pineapple pieces
- 2tbsp green onion,sliced
- ½tsp sesame seeds

INSTRUCTIONS

1. In a medium-sized bowl, consolidate prepared sauce fixings, nectar, rice vinegar, soy sauce, and tomato glue. Put away.

2. In a little bowl, consolidate the cornstarch and water.

3. Season pork with ½ teaspoon of salt and ¼ teaspoon of pepper.

4. In a shallow dish, combine as one flour and cornstarch.

5. In a different shallow dish, add eggs and whisk.

6. Batter each piece of pork by covering it with the flour blend then, at that point, plunge in the whisked egg, then, at that point, a last coat with the flour combination.

7. In a wok or medium-sized container, heat oil over medium-high warmth.

8. Once the oil arrives at 350 degrees F, work in 2 to 3 groups, adding the battered pork and broiling until brilliant brown and pork is cooked through for around 5 to 7 minutes.

9. Transfer pork to a sheet skillet and channel on paper towels. Fry the following cluster.

10. Discard the oil from the wok and cautiously wipe it within the skillet with paper towels to clean.

11. Heat the wok over medium-high warmth and include 1 tablespoon of oil.

12. Once the oil is hot, add the garlic and onions then, at that point, pan sear for 30 seconds.

13. Add in the red and green ringer peppers, and pan-fried food

for 1 moment.

14.   Add in the pineapple and sautéed food for 1 moment.

15.   Add in the pork and the prepared sauce, mix to join, and permit the sauce to reach boiling point.

16.   Stir the cornstarch slurry and afterward add it to the skillet, blending continually until the sauce thickens for around 60 seconds. Blend the fixings in with the sauce to cover the pork.

17.   Garnish the prepared pork with green onions and sesame seeds then, at that point, serve over rice.

10. Guinness Pulled Pork

Make your end-of-the-week informal breakfast additional uncommon with this pulled pork dish with a sweet and somewhat severe character from Guinness brew. Attempt it at home at this point.

Preparation:5 minutes

Cooking:10 hours

Total:10 hours 5 minutes

INGREDIENTS

- 1tbsp smoked paprika

- 2tsp salt

- 1tsp crushed red pepper

- ½tsp garlic powder

- ½tsp freshly broke dark pepper

- 4lb boneless pork butt

- 1 large white onion, thinly cut

- 1 bottleGuinness extra-bold lager

INSTRUCTIONS

1. In a little bowl, whisk together paprika, salt, squashed red pepper, garlic powder, and dark pepper until joined.

2. Rub the blend all around the outer layer of the pork until covered.

3. Spread out the cut onions over the lower part of the sluggish cooker. Then, at that point, place the pork on top. And afterward, pour the brew on top.

4. Cover and cook on Low for 10 to 12 hours, or until the pork self-destructs.

5. Serve on sliders, tacos, mixed greens, or any way you might want!

6. Store in an impermeable holder in the cooler for as long as four days, or freeze.

11. Fiery Pulled Pork

This pulled pork equation is moron evidence, tasty, and has a little kick of zing from the smoky adobo sauce and rich, full tomatoes!

Preparation:10 minutes

Cooking:6 hours 20 minutes

Total:6 hours 30 minutes

Fixings

- 1 medium onion
- 1tsp oregano, dried
- 2bay leaves, dried
- 1 chipotle
- 1 tbs padobo sauce
- 1 can tomatoes, squashed
- 1 can entire tomatoes in puree
- 2 tsp coarse salt
- ½ tsp ground pepper
- 2¾ lbs pork shoulder, boneless
- ·Flour tortillas
- cheddar cheddar, ground
- cream

Guidelines

1.   in a {very} extremely 5-quart slow cookware, join onion, oregano, bay leaves, chipotle, fish sauce, tomatoes, salt, and pepper. Add the pork; toss to cover with sauce.

2.   Cover, then, cook on a high setting for around six hours until the meat is pull-isolated fragile. imagine to not uncover though arrangement.

3.   Move meat to a goliath bowl; shred with forks, taking any tissue. return meat to pot, then, toss with sauce.

4.   To serve, get deter straight leaves; at whatever point required, decorate with tortillas and cheddar or sharp cream. Appreciate!

12. Vegan Jackfruit Force Pork

On the eater scene for quite whereas, jackfruit is gift else a typical individual from meatless weekday menus. Comparative in surface to force pork, unripe jackfruit absorbs regardless of getting ready you to feature combine in—with medical blessings needless to say.

Yet, suspend on a sec, jackfruit what? On the off likelihood that you simply} just haven't seen this before at Asian grocery stores or on the menu at your number one eater building, the jackfruit may be associate large tropical organic product that is remotely famed with figs. As indicated by the CA Rare Fruit Growers (CRFG), the jackfruit tree possibly came from Bharat, then, at that point, unfold throughout geographic region, the earth, and conjointly the

Philippines. lately it's likewise famed leaky, Brazil, and Surinam—and, for the on the so much aspect four to five years, in the U.S. As indicated by the CRFG, a solitary jackfruit can develop to eighty pounds (!) and quite xxxvi inches long and twenty creeps wide.

For this purpose, once the organic product is ready, it's totally sweet. In any case, the unripe organic product encompasses tons of unbiased, less sweet vogue, per the CRFG, and encompasses a surface among that "shreds" like force pork. there's a justification for why it's suddenly natural a really committed continuing among the plant-based native house.

Nonetheless, there is one major catch with jackfruit: it's relatively little or no macromolecule contrasted with different meat substitutes, says eater nutritionist Alex Caspero, R.D. One 75 gram (2.65-ounce) serving of plain jackfruit has only 1 gram of macromolecule (versus 10 grams of macromolecule in a {very} terribly similar living of tofu or twelve grams in an exceedingly very quarter cup of crude lentils). so don't anticipate that it have to be compelled to be your sole wellspring of macromolecule.

Making jackfruit force pork has never been simpler! the foremost ideal approach to serve it? A produce lover force pork sandwich. If you are doing not would love that, the alternatives area unit unending, and conjointly the BBQ jackfruit can get in tacos, on servings of mixed greens, and conjointly the sky is that the limit from there.

This is the right wedding between sweet, tart, and flavorsome and it will wow even the pickiest meat eater.

It is normally eater and sans super molecule, simply conceive to take under consideration but you serve it!

PREP TIME10 minutes

COOK TIME30 minutes

All out TIME40 minutes

INGREDIENTS

- 2 (20 ounces) jars of jackfruit (ideally not in saltwater)
- one onion slashed
- 5 cloves of garlic, minced
- 1.5 cups BBQ sauce (natively created or domestically acquired)
- 1/2 cup of water
- 2 teaspoons preserved paprika
- 1-2 tablespoons bean stew powder (to taste)
- one teaspoon cumin
- 2 teaspoons of salt
- one teaspoon of pepper

INSTRUCTIONS

1. In a {very} very screen, channel your jars of jackfruit and wash. subtract the exhausting aspects of the "hearts" that

you simply} just could feel on a bit of the things. simply just in case there is associate exhausting piece, it's perceptible once uptake the BBQ jackfruit so try to discontinue however exuberant you will be able to. Utilizing your hands or a fork, fine "shred" the jackfruit however exuberant you will be able to before preparation.

2. In a {very} very medium pan or pot over medium heat, saute your garlic and onion for around 5 minutes or until odoriferous.

3. Add among the jackfruit and conjointly the flavors ordinarily and saute for 2-3 minutes.

4. Pour in either do-it-yourself BBQ sauce domestically nurtural and conjointly the water. cowl with a chief and stew for 15-20 minutes.

5. subtract jackfruit from heat and utilizing a fork or a masher, shred the jackfruit to produce it the eater force pork look. you will shred it barely before preparation, however, this assists with the look and feel.

6. Come back jackfruit to the home appliance and switch the warmth up to high and eliminate the best. Let the abundance fluid bubble off and diminish for around 510 further minutes and you are finished!

7. Serve eater jackfruit force pork with eater coleslaw and on a breadstuff for a customary feast or attempt any choice you

will be able to imagine and appreciate.

13. Vegetarian pernil formula

Three staples in Puerto Rican food are rice, beans, and meat. One famous dish is broiled pork (pernil in Spanish). Jackfruit is a kind of natural product that has a surface like pork and chicken. This vegetarian pernil is flavorful and tastes very much like the meat adaptation! It's additionally very simple to make. Simply purchase canned pre-cut jackfruit, marinate it with this pernil marinade family formula, and dish it in the stove. This veggie lover pernil formula will fulfill your longings in general! It's so heavenly!

Fixings

- 2 containers vernal jackfruit
- 1 cup vegetable stock
- 5-6 tsp garlic cloves minaced
- 1/2 teaspoon oregano
- 1 tsp dish
- 1/2 tsp onion powder
- 1/4 tsp salt
- 1/8 tsp dim pepper

Guidelines

1. Channel the jackfruit from the craving and wash the off water.

2. Detect the marinade and jackfruit things in a {very} exceptionally plastic sack and seal the pack.

3. steep the jackfruit short among the cooler.

4. heat grill to 400°F.

5. Pour the jackfruit knots and marinade onto a preparing dish.

6. Spot among the grill and hotness for xxxv minutes or until fork-fragile compounding the vast majority of the in light of holding the things back from drying out.

7. Dispose of from the grill and let it sit for five minutes

8. gift related to your dear entremets or add it to a sandwich.

VEGAN CHICKEN RECIPES

1. Vegan Chicken Nuggets

For the best veggie lover chicken strips, skirt the store and attempt these natively constructed heated vegetarian chunks all things being equal. Seitan, frequently called "wheat meat," makes a shockingly meat-like vegetarian substitute for chicken in these fresh breaded tenders. You can make this simple formula with locally acquired or custommade seitan. Serve them up with your number one veggie lover plunging sauce.

In case you're desiring the kinds of chicken however you'd prefer to avoid the creature items, you will need to attempt our vegetarian chicken tender's formula. Our chunks are made with seitan (likewise now and again called "wheat meat") and a mix of flavors that gives them a shockingly chicken-like character. Then, at that point, they're prepared until fresh for plant-based treat children and grown-ups the same will cherish.

Prep time:10 mins

Cook time:50 mins

Complete time:1 hour

INGREDIENTS

- 1¾ cup indispensable wheat gluten
- 1-350g bundle of firm tofu, depleted and washed
- 1 20-ounce would young be able to green jackfruit in water or saline solution, depleted and washed and destroyed
- ⅔ cup no-chicken-style vegetable stock or bouillon, twofold strength
- 2 tbsp tahini
- 2 tsp ocean salt
- 2 tsp onion powder
- ¼ cup nutritional yeast
- ½ tsp fluid smoke
- 2 tbsp white miso glue
- 2 tsp poultry preparing
- 6-8 cups water, for cooking

INSTUCTIONS

1. To a rapid blender add tofu, no-chicken stock, tahini, ocean salt, onion powder, dietary yeast, poultry preparing, fluid smoke, and white miso glue. Mix on high until smooth.

2. Transfer to the bowl of a stand blender and add essential wheat gluten and destroyed jackfruit. Utilizing a level oar, ply on low speed until it meets up and begins to look like batter, around 3-5 minutes.

3. Stop and trade out the oar for a batter snare and massage at a low speed for 15-20 minutes. The batter will be delicate and marginally tacky with a sinewy surface. This is incredible for destroyed chicken. Assuming you need a more delicate chicken work for just 5ish minutes.

4. Divide fit the parts into an oval "log" and spot it in the focal point of a huge square of foil. Roll it tight, winding up the closures like wrapped sweets. Enclose by a second layer of foil and ensure everything is TIGHT. Rehash with the second "log".

5. Fill a tension cooker with 6-8 cups of water, and add both wrapped "logs".

6. Cook for 45 minutes under tension. On the off chance that you have a more modest strain cooker, you might need to do this in bunches.

7. Release the tension and eliminate the seitan rolls from the

cooker and let them cool totally.

8. (Alternatively, you can steam them for 60 minutes, on the off chance that you don't approach a tension cooker.)

9. Remove the logs from the foil and move them to a Tupperware compartment, and permit them to sit to permit the filaments to grow further.

10. Pull the seitan chicken into the chicken bosom or reduced down pieces, or shred and use marinades, flavors, or hitter to tweak the chicken to any dish.

2. Tofu Orange Chicken

This vegan tofu form has similar sweet and tart kinds to this customary Chinese chicken dish. The tofu is sauteed with garlic and afterward cooked in a combination of soy sauce, squeezed orange, rice vinegar, orange jelly, and ginger until the sauce is overall quite thick. Amazing served over rice. You could likewise attempt this formula with lumps of singed seitan for a chewier vegan artificial chicken formula.

Prep:10 mins

Cook:30 mins

Total:40 mins

Like Thai or Indonesian-style satays? Then, at that point, you will cherish this very simple veggie lover and vegetarian form of sound low-fat tofu prepared in a flavorful Thaienlivened nut sauce. We love pretty much any sort of prepared tofu, however, this must be one of our top picks.

Serve it over rice and feel free to add the extras to a vegetable sautéed food with noodles briefly feast. It turned out something somewhat like this tofu and broccoli pan sear with nut sauce.

This prepared tofu makes for a basic principle dish, or add it to servings of mixed greens, sautés, or noodles. It's veggie-lover, vegetarian and on the off chance that you utilize a sans gluten soy sauce, for example, tamari, it's without gluten too.

INGREDIENTS

- 1 (12-to 14-ounce) square of tofu, firm or additional firm
- 1/4 cup peanut butter, rich or normal peanut butter is ideal (no lumps)
- 1/2 teaspoon ground ginger

- 2 tablespoons lime juice, or squeezed orange

- 1 tablespoon soy sauce

- 2 tablespoons sesame oil (olive oil can be utilized in case you're after all other options have been exhausted)

- 3 tablespoons maple syrup, nectar, or agave nectar

- 1 tablespoon sweet bean stew sauce

INSTRUCTIONS

1. Gather the ingredients.

2. First, press your bean curd.

3. Once your bean curd is incredibly a lot of squeezed, cut it into your ideal shapes. Flimsy sections, triangles, or maybe very little scaled-down shapes can work.

4. Once your bean curd is set, pre-heat the stove to four hundred F. Line a getting ready plate with tin foil on the off likelihood that you just will since heated bean curd currently and once more gets somewhat tacky, and therefore the foil makes order easy.

5. Next, established the sauce. Whisk along the spread (soften it somewhat within the microwave for less than a few of moments to create this simpler) with the ginger, juice or squeezed orange, soy sauce, sesame oil, syrup, and sweet bean stew sauce. Before you prepare your bean curd, provide the sauce a quick style. It have to be compelled to

be heavenly. If not, amendment the flavors to style.

6. Coat the bean curd with the nut sauce on all sides. you'll move the sauce to a good shallow bowl or dish and dunk it in, or utilize a cake brush to hide each bit the arduous method just in case you are operating with larger components of bean curd. we tend to prefer to plunge it, then, at that time, surface extra sauce.

7. Bake the bean curd on the stove for around fifteen to seventeen minutes, observation out for them in order that they do not consume. flip items over, and prepare a new ten to fifteen minutes. (Note: The sauce on the tin foil can consume a touch, relax. you just do not have any want to ascertain the coated bean curd consume.)

8. Serve and appreciate!

3. Hot Seitan Buffalo "Wings"

Vegetarian Buffalo wings are frequently pre-arranged similarly to once using genuine chicken. The chicken substitute seitan is roofed with flavors, burned, and later tossed with spread and sauce. These veggie-sweetheart Buffalo wings are very wooly, genuinely actually like the genuine article, subsequently gift with a lot of napkins! you'll similarly assemble this dish using bean curd.

Prep:10 minutes

Cook:10 minutes

Total:20 minutes

Red hot seitan bovid "wings" are a green basic foods sweetheart and eater substitute for commonplace bar Buffalo wings by and by with generally speaking comparable flavors and flavor and scorched goodness covered in melty spread (guarantee its eater spread if important!) and hot wing sauce, an extraordinary arrangement very much like the underlying Buffalo wings made exploitation chicken. It's really disturbing the sauce. We've made this equation with a couple of differed kinds of sauce, by the by as a last resort, Frank's wiener Original Dish Sauce is partner praiseworthy call. We're eventually an admirer for a couple of reasons, nonetheless, one defense is that it's extraordinarily low in sugar and it doesn't have any additional high organic product sugar syrup.

Goodness, and since it's radiant!

Seitan doesn't go with wings to any degree farther than bovid do, by and by these meatless Buffalo wings are prepared with sauce and spread for a closely resembling fiery person. in the event you are a green staple goods darling or eater World Health Organization Misses Buffalo wings (or knows about somebody World Health Organization does), you may not be disillusioned with this equation!

Need a protein eater hot wing thought? attempt this transformation of green staple goods darling hot wings made with bean curd, or save for, on the off probability that you just can't get satisfactory veggie-sweetheart wing considerations, attempt these Chinese benne "chicken" wings or these eater cauliflower bovid wings - yum!

INGREDIENTS

- one-pound seitan, dig strips
- a pair of teaspoon garlic powder
- one teaspoon onion powder
- Oil, for broil
- 1/3 cup spread, dissolved
- 1/2 cup sauce, or wing sauce like Frank's hotdog Wing Sauce

INSTRUCTIONS

1. First, cowl your cleaved seitan with garlic powder and onion powder. then, at that time, gently fry in edible fat or oil over medium-high heat for five to seven minutes, or till daintily grilled on all sides.

2. in a very medium-sized bowl, mix jointly the liquefied spread and sauce.

3. Place the seitan within the bowl and blend to hide well.

4. The covering with fix up because it cools, departure you with a flavorous, coated seitan dish that is equally as regards to as tacky and pleasant because the real article. Appreciate!

4. Velvety vegan Chicken and Rice

You don't should be partner omnivore to discover the value in a sublime dish of relieving "chicken" and rice. an incredible arrangement actually like the ordinary transformation, this eater pleasant recipe is brimming with smooth sauce even as lively vegetables and bean curd for the surface. an ideal shock of energy for a fresh evening.

This recipe is regularly pre-arranged early and frozen as well. To thaw out, principally heat in a very container (close by a dash of non-dairy milk) till it shows up at the best temperature.

Prep:30 minutes

Cook:30 minutes

Total:60 minutes

Fixings

For Rice:

- a pair of cups natural hued rice
- a pair of teaspoons vegetable stock
- five cups of water

For Sauce:

- one 3D structure or teaspoon chicken-prepared vegetable stock

- 1/2 teaspoon authentic salt

- a pair of to three tablespoons dietary yeast

- one block extra-firm rich bean curd

For Tofu:

- one block extra-firm bean curd

- one tablespoon vegetable oil

- one tablespoon new astute, minced

- one tablespoon rosemary, minced

- Kosher salt, to taste

For vegetables:

- one tablespoon vegetable oil

- a pair of cups hacked portobello mushrooms

- 1/2 cup diced carrot

- one cup hacked asparagus

- Kosher salt, to taste

Guidelines

1. Gather the fixings.

2. Preheat oven to 375 F. Encase tofu with an ideal drying towel and detect a plate on top. Recognize a generous can or equivalent thing on top of the plate to trouble it, and let channel for 20 minutes.

3. Add 2 strong states of vegetable bouillon to 5 cups water.

4. Cook rice according to package direction, using vegetable bouillon.

5. Heat a tablespoon of olive oil in an enormous skillet over medium-low warmth, then, add vegetables.

6. Cover and cook until carrots are fragile, salt to taste, then, set aside until arranged to use.

7. Slice tofu around 1/2-inch thick. Join olive oil and adroit as one and brush onto tofu cuts, then, move to a delicately lubed warming sheet.

8. Roast tofu for around 30 minutes or until firm and cooked on the different sides. Dispose of from the oven, let cool, then, cut into diminished down pieces.

9. Make the sauce by merging bouillon, salt, sustaining yeast, and sumptuous tofu in a food processor. Blend until particularly smooth. Set aside.

10. Once the rice is finished cooking, merge everything along close by rice. Warm on low warmth if vital. Serve hot.

11. Formula Variation

12. Add a 1/2 square of smooth tofu, 1 tablespoon supporting yeast, and 1/2 strong shape more bouillon expecting you need the dish to be extra smooth.

5. Vegan "Chicken" Pot Pie with Garden

For a veggie dear and vegetarian pot pie focal dish, attempt this fundamental particularly planned veggie-darling pot pie condition piled up with veggie darling Garden "chicken" scaloppini, onions, carrots, and green peas and prepared into a ramekin with thyme, sage, and other scrumptious flavors all covered with a light and flaky puff arranged incredible. You'll see that this veggie darling pot pie with vegetarian chicken is equivalently as liberal and filling as some other pot pie yet much lower in fat and totally without cholesterol.

Prep:20 mins

Cook:35 mins

Total:55 mins

Decorations

- 1 bundle veggie lover chicken substitute (like Gardein chicken scallopini), cut into 1/4-inch strong shapes

- 2 to 4 tablespoons canola oil, bound

- 3/4 teaspoon sea salt

- 3/4 teaspoon dull pepper

- 3/4 cup veggie-dear margarine

- 3/4 cup regularly significant flour

- 6 cups veggie-dear chicken stock

- 1 cup yellow onion, diced

- 1 cup carrots, stripped and diced

- 3/4 teaspoon thyme, minced

- 3/4 teaspoon sage, minced

- 1 tablespoon dietary yeast pieces

- 1 tablespoon tamari

- 1 cup green peas

- 1 sheet veggie-dear puff warmed unprecedented, done to 12 x 10 inches

Rules

1. Gather the designs. Preheat grill to 375 F.

2. Brown the cut Gardein scallopini in a sautee holder with 1 tablespoon of the canola oil. Season with a bit (around 1/4 teaspoon each one) of salt and pepper. Dispose of from the dish and set aside.

3. To make a roux, separate the vegan margarine in a saute holder, add flour, and whisk unendingly until light brown in covering. Cool and set aside.

4. In a huge soup or stockpot, heat the veggie sweetheart chicken stock until carefully stewing. Keep this stewing and hot for the going with stage.

5. In a 5.5-quart stockpot, cook onions in canola oil for 3 minutes

and add carrots, sage, and thyme, close by the rest of the salt and pepper. Continue to cook for 5 minutes. Add the now stewing vegetable stock and stew for 5 minutes. Speed in drawing in yeast chips.

6. Add the set up margarine and flour roux a piece instantly, to cook as the sauce thickens. Blend in the Gardein scallopini, tamari, and peas. Void mix into a tremendous shallow holder to cool.

7. Right when the mix is cool, fill individual ramekins, a glass pie holder, or a little feast dish. Cover mix in with puff masterminded phenomenal (try to leave fairly bounty of cake for falling and fluting of the edge), and seal edges. Cut little cuts. Hotness for 35 min or until inside temperature shows up at 165 F.

8. Right when the mix is cool, fill individual ramekins, a glass pie compartment, or a little dinner dish. Cover blend in with puff warmed extraordinary (attempt to leave fairly excess of cake for falling and fluting of the edge), and seal edges. Cut little cuts. Hotness for 35 min or until internal temperature shows up at 165F.

6. Vegetarian Tempeh "Chicken" Salad

A veggie darling "chicken" salad equation made with tempeh as a veggie sweetheart and vegan chicken substitute. Make it a veggie-sweetheart by using a sans egg and without dairy vegan mayonnaise as opposed to standard mayonnaise; all of the various trimmings is veggie lover. Another other option? To change this tempeh salad into a direct curried tempeh chicken serving of blended greens, incorporate an unobtrusive bundle of raisins and divided almonds and addition the proportion of curry, perhaps adding a dab more salt too.

All things considered like a standard chicken plate of blended greens equation, this vegetarian tempeh chicken plate of blended greens recipe is one of those plans that will do best made early, so it has a great deal of time to chill in the cooler, allowing the tempeh to ingest all of the flavors.

Prep:20 mins

Cook:10 mins

Total:20 mins

Decorations

- 1 pack tempeh (cut into 1/2-inch 3D squares)

- Water for warming the tempeh

- 2 tablespoons olive oil

- 3 tablespoons mayonnaise or veggie dear mayonnaise

- 2 teaspoons lemon juice

- 2 tablespoons onion (minced)

- 3 stems celery (minced)

- 1 tablespoon dried parsley

- 1/4 teaspoon curry powder

- Optional: a scramble of cayenne pepper

Rules

1. Gather the trimmings.

2. Bring a couple of crawls of water to an air pocket in a pot or huge skillet. Add the cut tempeh. Stew for 15 minutes. Channel.

3. NOTE: Tempeh should be cooked first—it can't be utilized harsh, regardless of the way that it will ultimately be served chilled.

4. Heat two tablespoons of olive oil over medium warmth. Add tempeh and fry for around 5 minutes, blending as consistently as possible to cook on all sides. Discard the skillet from warmth and award it to cool.

5. In a huge bowl, join the cooled tempeh with mayonnaise or veggie sweetheart mayonnaise, lemon juice, onion, celery, dried parsley, curry powder, and cayenne pepper. Mix to combine well, ensuring that the mayonnaise blend reliably

covers the tempeh.

6. Season tenderly with salt and pepper. Taste, and change flavors or add somewhat more salt and pepper to taste, in the event that you'd like.

7. Enjoy your tempeh chicken serving of mixed greens on a bed of lettuce, between two carefully toasted cuts of bread or stuffed into pita bread for a pocket pita sandwich.

Formula Variations

fuse an unassuming heap of raisins and isolated almonds and expansion the extent of curry to make a curried tempeh chicken serving of mixed greens

7. Vegetarian Cashew "Chicken" Stir Fry

Like cashew chicken? Need an Asian-stirred container singe recipe with a bit of crunch? Endeavor this veggie darling and vegan container singe with bamboo shoots, celery, and cashews close by tofu and a ton of vegetables.

On the off chance that you've never used bamboo shoots in vegetable seared food, you're in for a shock. If you see them fairly woody and as too hard to even think about evening consider gnawing, cut them the long way; they're too fat coming directly from the can. Be that as it may, make an effort not to be reluctant to endeavor them. While they are a customary Chinese fixing, they have significantly milder taste diverged from other Chinese trimmings that Westerners might possibly like, for instance, hoisin sauce and wood ear mushrooms.

Prep:10 mins

Cook:15 mins

Total:25 mins

Fixings

- 2 tablespoons nut oil (or vegetable oil)

- 2-3 cloves garlic (minced)

- 1 teaspoon new ginger (minced)

- 8 ounces firm (or extra-firm) tofu (generally crushed)

- 3/4 cup mushrooms (cut)

- 1 (4-ounce) can bamboo shoots (exhausted and undeniably cut thin)

- 2 stems celery (cut)

- 1 red (or green) ring pepper (hacked)

- 1/3 cup vegetable stock (or water)

- 2 tablespoons soy sauce

- 1 tablespoon cornstarch (mixed in with 3 tablespoons water)

- 1/2 cup cashews

- Discretionary: 3 green onions (divided)

Guidelines

1. In a colossal skillet or wok, heat the oil and add garlic and ginger for one short time, then, add the tofu, carefully mixing to work up the ginger and garlic. Warmth for 3 to 4 minutes, until tofu is delicately splendid.

2. Add the red ringer pepper and celery and warmth, mixing, for about a second, then, add the mushrooms and bamboo shoots.

3. Add the vegetable stock or water and soy sauce and license to stew for another short time, until vegetables are sensitive anyway not yet done.

4. Mix in the water-cornstarch mix, heat until thickened and vegetables are done cooking; then, blend in cashews and green onions. Join well.

5. Serve this vegetable sautéed food speedily with steamed rice, cooked noodles, or your main whole grain

8. Seitan Fried "Chicken" Tenders

This veggie darling "chicken" dish is southern style and amazingly tasty. Sautéed seitan and a mix of flavors make a dish that is amazingly close plainly and taste to burned chicken. The dish gets together rapidly, with no marinating time key.

Buying planned seitan will obstruct any time expected to make the protein out of central wheat gluten and flavors. Seitan is accessible in tangles, solid shapes, cuts, and steaks. For this situation, you can buy the bunches for piece assessed bits of consumed "chicken," or cut the steaks an upward way with the target that they are formed like long chicken fingers.

For best outcomes with the covering, utilize a veggie darling egg thing like Just Eggs or Follow Your Heart that copies the full volume of eggs.

Prep:15 mins

Cook:15 mins

Marinate:60 mins

Total:90 mins

Trimmings

- 1 1/2 cups regularly accommodating (wheat or sans gluten mix) flour

- 2 teaspoons garlic powder

- 2 teaspoons sweet paprika

- 2 teaspoon onion powder

- 1 teaspoon dried thyme

- 1 teaspoon dried oregano

- 1 teaspoon celery salt

- 1/2 teaspoon ground dull pepper

- 1/2 teaspoon dried scoured sage

- 1 pound seitan (steaks cut into tenders or pieces)

- 1 cup coordinated veggie-sweetheart egg replacer

- Neutral oil, like sunflower, adequate for critical consuming

Bearings

1. Collect the trimmings.

2. Mix the flour and flavors in a medium-assessed blending bowl.

3. Spot egg replacer in a shallow bowl and set up a tunneling station of the coordinated flour, egg replacer, and seitan pieces.

4. Delve seitan pieces in the flour, then, at that point, dunk them in the egg replacer, then, at that point, jump them back into the flour once more. Press delicately if significant so that there is a strong external covering of flour.

Hotness oil over medium-high warmth in a colossal skillet until it appears at 375 degrees.

6. Fry lumps of "chicken" in the oil on medium-high warmth in a huge skillet for 1/2 to 2 minutes for each side, until the various sides are stunning brown. Channel pieces once killed from the compartment and present with veggie darling residence dressing, vegetarian tarter sauce, or veggie dear soy plunging sauce.

9. Veggie lover Chinese Kung Pao Tofu

In spite of the way that kung pao is conventionally made with chicken, you can utilize tofu to make an on an exceptionally essential level a comparative veggie darling and vegetarian change of this Chinese Szechuan dish. All of similar flavors is utilized, including sesame oil, red pepper pieces, soy sauce, and garlic, making a hot and heavenly sauce. This veggie dear kung pao tofu condition comparatively calls for heaps of sound vegetables including snow peas, bok choy, cabbage, and mushrooms, making for an astonishing and nutritious dish. Serve this Szechuan-style Chinese kung pao tofu formula over rice.

Standard kung pao plans are extremely hot and combine stew peppers and

Szechuan peppercorns. This variety uses red pepper drops and hot sauce to develop some shine, regardless, go ahead and utilize the peppers on the off chance that you like.

Prep:45 mins

Cook:15 mins

Total:60 mins

Trimmings

1 pound firm or additional firm tofu (squeezed and cut into scaled back 3D shapes)

For the Marinade:

- 3 tablespoons vegetable stock

- 1 tablespoon as of late pressed lime juice

- 2 tablespoons soy sauce (or tamari to keep it without gluten)

- 1 tablespoon sesame oil

For the Stir-Fry:

- 2 tablespoons sesame oil

- 1 medium onion (diced)

- 1 red cost pepper (diced)

- 1/4 teaspoon red pepper pieces

- 1/2 cup cut mushrooms

- 1 tablespoon minced new ginger

- 1 little bok choy (cut)

- 1/4 cup vegetable stock

- 1/2 cup snow peas

- 1/2 insignificant purple cabbage (cut unimposing)

- 1 tablespoon cut new parsley

- 1 teaspoon hot sauce

- Salt and pepper to taste

Headings

1. Marinate and Bake the Tofu

2. Gather the tofu and marinade decorations.

3. Make the marinade: Combine the vegetable stock, lime juice, soy sauce, and sesame oil in a bowl.

4. Add the tofu and award to marinate for no under 30 minutes, blending now and again to cover the tofu well.

5. Preheat the stove to 375 F. Oil an arranging sheet or cover with aluminum foil.

6. Bake the tofu for 15 minutes, turning once. Put away.

7. Cook the Stir-Fry

8. Gather the plenitude decorations.

9. In a huge skillet or wok over medium-high warmth, heat the sesame oil.

10. Add the onion, ringer pepper, red pepper chips, mushrooms, and ginger and saute for 3 to 5 minutes, blending consistently.

11. Add bok choy and vegetable stock and cook for 3 to 5 additional minutes.

12. Add the cabbage and snow peas.

13. Reduce the gleam to low and add the tofu and remaining decorations.

Cook until just until joined together and warmed through.

Tips

- Like most vegan tofu plans, this tofu condition will taste best in the event that you press the tofu first. This permits the tofu to hold a more unmistakable proportion of the flavorings and flavors it is cooked with.

- If you need this condition to be sans gluten comparably as a veggie-darling, use tamari instead of the soy sauce and twofold check that your vegetable stock is without gluten.

- Sesame oil has a lower smoke point stood apart from vegetable oil, so be mindful when warming it up so it doesn't consume.

10. Orange Glazed Tempeh

Like the orange chicken, you get at Chinese cafés? Need to attempt a vegan form at home? One of the insider facts which numerous veggie lovers and vegetarians know is that reproducing most suppers has very little to do with the actual meat. All things considered, the main thing about Chinese eatery-style orange chicken truly isn't the chicken - it's the sweet and tart orange coating that makes the dish.

Along these lines, this formula joins every one of the elements of the orange coating and puts it on an incredible veggie-lover meat substitute - tempeh - rather than chicken. The formula calls for new squeezed orange (it actually should be new for this formula - don't utilize concentrate or frozen!), maple syrup for pleasantness, soy sauce for pungency, and a couple of different flavors too.

You can serve this orange tempeh over rice or pretty much some other entire grain, or then again, on the off chance that you'd like more a rounder supper, you can twofold the coating fixings and include some steamed veggies too - attempt snow peas, child corn, and ringer peppers to keep it Asian-themed, or even broccoli or bok choy, or pretty much anything, truly. Cauliflower may be pleasant as well.

Prep:20 mins

Cook:15 mins

Total:35 mins

INGREDIENTS

- 1 4-ounce bundle tempeh, cut into 3/4-inch 3D squares
- 2 cups new crushed squeezed orange
- 1/4 cup maple syrup
- 4 teaspoons soy sauce
- 1 teaspoon ground coriander
- 1 teaspoon ground ginger
- 2 carrots, stripped and cut into 1-inch pieces
- 1 tablespoon vegetable oil
- 4 cups cooked blended wild and earthy colored rice
- 2 tablespoons new cilantro, cleaved

INSTRUCTIONS

1. In a bowl, whisk together squeezed orange, maple syrup, soy sauce, coriander, and ginger. Stew carrots in daintily salted water for around 10 minutes or until delicate; channel.

2. In another pot; bubble tempeh in unsalted water for 10 minutes; channel and wipe off.

3. In a huge skillet, heat oil over medium warmth. Add tempeh and brown on all sides. Add carrots and squeezed orange blend and stew until fluid is a sweet coating. To serve, spoon tempeh and coat over rice; sprinkle with cilantro.

Tips

- Need it to be without gluten? Tempeh is frequently - yet not generally - without gluten, so make certain

- to choose tempeh that is altogether sans protein, if necessary, and trade out the quality soy for a while not protein tamari, or, you'll even utilize coconut aminos or Bragg's fluid amino. The leftover fixings square measure all while not protein.

- Need it to be a full vegetarian feast? Serve your Chinese-propelled tempeh "chicken" with Chinese scallion hotcakes or the perfect rice.

11. veggie sweetheart Moroccan-style "chicken" stew

Vegan Moroccan-Style "Chicken" Stew, using plant-based macromolecule or warmed bean curd, riffs off accessory degree commendable dish stacked with veggies and fragrant with punch. This exquisite smelling stew might be an amazing thinking to share inside the brand name flavors and partitions of Moroccan food— including carrots, tomatoes, dried standard thing, chickpeas, and cinnamon

Overriding the chicken commonly utilized during this stew isn't infuriating to try to — use a store of formed plant-based chicken-style macromolecule or go a gigantic heap of standard with warmed bean curd or chicken-style seitan.

This dish is by and large served over couscous, yet I propose quinoa as a colossal heap of dumbfounding and higher-protein elective. On the other hand aside from, you'll have the decision to stop poached grains absolutely and gift with new bread.

Prep time20 minutes

Cook time30 minutes

Overall time50 minutes

Decorations

- two tablespoons extra-virgin vegetable oil, allotted

- eight to twelve ounces' chicken-style plant macromolecule or orchestrated bean curd, turn over downsized strips

- one marvelous purple onion, confined

- two to three cloves garlic, minced

- two cups water

- one extraordinary or two medium sweet potatoes, stripped and turn more than 3/4 in. projections

- four medium carrots, stripped and cut around 1/4 in. thick

- 15-ounce will have diced fire-scorched tomatoes, undrained

- 15-ounce will chickpeas, exhausted and washed

- two teaspoons ground cumin

- one teaspoon ground cinnamon

- 1/2 teaspoon ground turmeric

- 3/4 cup dried apricots, truncate the middle

- 1/2 cup remove new parsley, isolated

- Salt and new ground pepper to style

- Cooked couscous or quinoa, optional

Headings

1. Hotness one tablespoon of the oil during a soup pot. Add the plant-based chicken or masterminded bean curd and sauté over medium hotness till exceptional brown on most sides. Move to a bowl or plate and spot away.

2. during a relative pot, heat the bounty oil. Add the onion and sauté over medium hotness till clear. Add the garlic and continue to sauté till the onion is satisfactory.

3. Add the water, followed by the sweet potatoes, carrots, tomatoes, chickpeas, cumin, cinnamon, and turmeric. mix an indifferent air pocket, then, at that point, around then, cut down the hotness. cowl and stew fine for quarter-hour, or till the vegetables square measure tricky.

4. Mix inside the chicken or masterminded bean curd, apricots, and an outsized piece of the parsley. Season with salt and pepper and stew over strikingly low hotness for five to ten minutes longer.

5. In the event that serving while not poached grain, in a general sense scoop into shallow dishes. in the event you are going with the grains, place an unassuming extent of poached couscous

or quinoa inside the dishes first, followed by the stew. Notwithstanding, sprinkle each giving the extra parsley.

12. vegetarian general Tso's chicken

This sweet and red hot veggie lover General Tso's Chicken might be a scrumptious veganized Chinese takeout breathed life into dish. Sans protein and stacked with flavor!

Fixings

- Vegetarian Chicken
- eight oz soy turns
- one ¾ cups vegetable stock or water
- eight oz broccolini or broccoli, cut in 1" things
- one medium red toll pepper, cut
- three cloves garlic, cut, optional
- poached rice, unpracticed onions, and herbaceous plant seeds, for serving
- Veggie sweetheart General Tso's Sauce
- 1-2 tablespoon new ground ginger, to taste
- three cloves garlic, minced or ground
- ½ cup unseasoned rice vinegar
- ½ cup decreased metal soy (use gf tamari or no-soy if vital)
- ½ cup coconut sugar

- two tablespoon hoisin (use sans protein if important)

- ½ teaspoon smoke-dried paprika

- ½ teaspoon red pepper things, to taste

- ½ cup water

- two tablespoon arrowroot powder or corn flour

Directions

1.　Note concerning veggies: I favor to sauté the vegetables first and a while later add them back in toward the tip, that strategy they need a legit surface to them and don't get excessively delicate with all the contrary things - in any case, move and cook the vegetables however you see work.

2.　Cook veggies: In an enormous elusive pot over medium-high hotness, add the cut garlic if using, cook 1-3 minutes till pleasant smelling and clear, including water or stock a made to order premise (clearly you might cook with oil on the off likelihood that you actually like). Then, at that point, around then, add your veggies. As to such an extent as i'd anguish, I cooked the broccoli for around five minutes however NOT the red ringer pepper since I slant toward my red toll peppers fresh, not fragile. I place a shelter on for a lump of these five minutes to direct the broccoli somewhat steaming action. Cook according to your tendencies. Regardless, remove your poached veggies from the pot and spot them during a bowl, and shelter either with a piece plate or foil.

3.   Rehydrate soy turns if using: though your veggies square measure cookery, rehydrate the soy turns by swing them during a medium bowl and adding vegetable stock or water with incredible consideration the most noteworthy soy contorts square measure floating exclusively a little endless sum, as to such an extent as I'd struggle, around one ¾ cups stock for eight oz. soy turns. It must be constrained to hold all the water in around 6-8 minutes, be that as it may, in the event that it doesn't, the channel of the water a lengthy time before cookery them.

4.   Sauté garlic and ginger: Sauté the minced or ground ginger and garlic next over medium-high hotness for around 1-2 minutes or till aromatic in your great elusive pot. actually look at that to highlight a smidgen of water or stock to convey them back from remaining.

5.   Earthy colored soy turns: right now, add the (exhausted if essential) soy turns to your pot and change around the hotness to high. Cook them for around 5-7 minutes, intermixture just a single time in a very while. you might want to prompt a touch hearty hued tone on the soy turns.

6.   Add sauce trimmings: as of now add your elective sauce trimmings to a touch bowl or assessing cup: rice vinegar, soy sauce/GF tamari/No Soy, duck sauce, coconut sugar, smoke-dried paprika, and red pepper things. Speed till joined and fill the pot. join well and produce to a high stew. This just took several second for the benefit of me.

7. Thicken: in a tiny bowl or instrumentality, race along the water and arrowroot powder or amylum till it is a wash suspension. Void it into the pot and mix in well. it'll thicken inside 30-60 seconds. you'll have the option to stay with it change of state it on medium on the off chance that you'd like better to cook down the sauce fundamentally any, regardless I didn't need to on the grounds that it was appallingly thick and cheap.

8. Add back veggies: presently add the vegetables back in to instigate them hot again and covered inside the sauce, around 1-2 minutes. Wipe out heat.

9. Serve: Serve with medium rice at whatever point required and high with unpracticed onions, spice seeds, and extra red pepper drops on the off chance that you might want. Appreciate!

10. Store: Refrigerate additional items in an extremely fixed shut compartment for up to five days or freeze in an exceptionally cooler safe holder for up to ninety days.

Veggie lover BEEF RECIPES

1."Beef" Stroganoff with veggie lover Substitute

Throbbing for the sort of old-school burger stroganoff, in any case have stayed away from meat? Fear not, there is a system to share during this liberal, standard dish though holding fast to a green product darling or eater diet.

This handsewn green merchandise sweetheart "meat" stroganoff starts with territorially no inheritable vegan "burger," that is then caramelized with onions and mushrooms. the blend is medium in an extremely speedy sauce of canned cream of mushroom soup and sharp cream, similarly as a standard stroganoff made with meat would be ready.

Gardein brand's beefless tips region unit arranged, regardless you'll have the option to use any meat substitute you wish or attempt only using standard seitan. On the off likelihood that you essentially use seitan, you should brown it delicately on all sides for an incredible about six to seven minutes included. what is extra, promise it's cut into downsized things. Prep:5 minutes

Cook:20 minutes

Total:25 minutes

Fixings

- one tablespoon oil

- nine ounces veggie-sweetheart meat substitute (like Gardein Beefless Tips)

- one very little onion, diced

- eight ounces cremini mushrooms, cut

- one clove garlic, minced

- one (15-ounce) will cream of mushroom soup

- three tablespoons brutal cream

- 1/2 cup dry vino

- one tablespoon finely sliced new parsley

- two cups medium level noodles

Directions

1. Accumulate the fixings.

2. Hotness oil in an exceptionally medium sauté skillet and delicately gritty hued vegan "burger" on all sides. this could take around about six to seven minutes. Dependent upon which sort of meat substitute you are using, be cautious for it along these lines it doesn't devour.

3. Add onions, mushrooms, and garlic to the instrumentality and stick with it change of state for around three minutes longer.

4. Add cream of mushroom soup and brutal cream, intermixture to merge well.

5. Mix in vino and cook for a further ten minutes, blending some of the time. you will similarly must be constrained to decrease the fieriness of a lump to a medium-low.

6. When everything is absolutely medium, sprinkle with parsley and serve veggie lover "meat" stroganoff on high of medium noodles.

2. veggie dear meat pie with Plant-Based Meat

This condition gives an admirable solace food a plant-based makeover. Shepherd's pie is a sensible stray pieces dish, for which a thick layer of smooth pureed potatoes is prepared over a filling of ground sheep or meat, carrots, and peas in a tomato-showed up at sauce.

In this grouping, we trade the ground meat for a plant-based meat elective. This condition will work best with one, for example, Beyond or Impossible that are sold "unforgiving," sending an impression of taking after ground meat, then, at that point, sautéed on the burner, versus those that are sold pre-cooked. By sautéing the "meat" inside the occasion, you're ready to lace the pie's flavors, like thyme and rosemary, more basically than with a pre-cooked arrangement.

Prep:40 mins

Cook:30 mins

Total:70 mins

Upgrades

For the Mashed Potatoes:

- 4 cups stripped and 3/4-inch-diced potatoes

- 4 tablespoons veggie dear spread or margarine

- 1/4 cup veggie dear cream

- 1 teaspoon salt

- 1/8 teaspoon ground dull pepper

- 1/2 cup veggie dear sharp cream

- 1/4 cup ground veggie dear Parmesan **For the**

Filling:

- 1 tablespoon sensible oil, for example, grapeseed oil or avocado oil

- 1 cup diced onion

- 1 cup diced carrot

- 1-pound plant-based meat, for example, Beyond or Impossible

- 1 teaspoon dried thyme

- 1 teaspoon dried rosemary

- 2 tablespoons all around solid flour

- 2 tablespoons tomato stick

- 1 tablespoon veggie dear Worcestershire sauce

- 1 tablespoon soy sauce

- 1 cup no-chicken stock

- 1/2 teaspoon salt

- 1/4 teaspoon ground faint pepper

- 3/4 cup frozen peas, defrosted

Headings

Note: while there are various strides to the current situation, this dish is segregated into significant classes to assist you with bettering approach for designing and cooking.

Make the Potatoes

1. Gather the upgrades.

2. Add potatoes to an epic pot of cool water, cover, and hotness to the clarification in climbing over high hotness. While frothing, reduction to medium-low, discard the cover, and stew until potatoes are fork-delicate, around 12 minutes.

3. Drain potatoes in a colander, then, at that point, return to the pot and add margarine, creamer or flavor, salt, and pepper. Pound until no enormous packs remain.

4. Add fierce cream and parmesan, mix absolutely to wire, and save.

Make the Filling

Collect the plans.

Perceive an epic dish over medium-high hotness and add oil. Once hot, sauté the onion and carrot until the onion is clear, around 4 minutes.

Add ruthless ground "meat," nearby thyme and rosemary, and sauté until singed and cooked through; this might change subject to the brand, so stick to the pack headings. (It will usually not need over 10 minutes.)

Sprinkle flour over the blend and sauté for 30 seconds while mixing, until all upgrades are covered.

Add tomato stick, Worcestershire sauce, soy sauce, stock, salt, and pepper, and mix well to join.

While muttering, decline hotness to medium-low and stew for 3 minutes, until the sauce has thickened barely.

Add frozen peas, blending them in totally, and shed filling from heat.

3. Veggie lover Impossible Swedish "Meatballs"

These warm and calming Swedish meatballs are absolutely flavorful while being absolutely veggie sweetheart! We used Impossible Burger ground "cheeseburger," by and by available in various grocery stores, to make the meatballs . No one will really need to tell that the dish doesn't use authentic meat, since Impossible takes after and has a character like burger. The sauce is made with coconut milk, making it rich and smooth with no dairy. Serve this equation to any veggie sweetheart or meat eater and they make sure to be fulfilled.

Serve the meatballs on a bed of rich pureed potatoes or with cauliflower rice on the off chance that you're looking for less carbs. A little lingonberry jam as a bit of hindsight is furthermore an undeniable necessity.

Prep:15 mins

Cook:20 mins

Total:35 mins

Trimmings

For the Meatballs:

- 1 pound Impossible Burger meat

- 1/2 sweet onion, finely minced

- 1/2 cup panko breadcrumbs

- 2 tablespoons coconut milk

- 1 teaspoon healthy yeast

- 1 teaspoon onion powder

- 1 teaspoon garlic powder

- 1/2 teaspoon fit salt

- 1/2 teaspoon dull pepper

- 1/4 cup olive oil

Rules

Note: while there are various steps to this recipe, this dish is isolated into useful classes to help you with bettering plan for preparation and cooking.

Make the Meatballs

1. Gather the trimmings.

2. Add the meat, sliced onions, and breadcrumbs to a huge bowl. Pour the coconut milk over the most elevated mark of the breadcrumbs. License the breadcrumbs to assimilate the milk.

3. Add the healthy yeast, onion powder, garlic powder, salt, and pepper to the meat mix and mix to combine and absolutely disperse the flavors.

4. Use a little treat scoop to shape the meat mix into 1-inch size balls. Spot them on a material lined getting ready sheet and continue rolling and outlining until they are completely wrapped up.

5. Hotness the olive oil in a gigantic sauté holder on medium-high hotness. Add the meatballs to the skillet and cook on one side for around 1 second. Turn and cook on each side until sautéed (for an amount of around 5 minutes).

6. Kill the meatballs from the skillet and spot them on a plate. Set up the sauce.

Make the Gravy

1. Gather the trimmings.

2. Add the veggie sweetheart spread to the dish used for sautéing the meatballs and return to medium-high hotness. Race in the flour and grant to cook for two minutes, blending from time to time. Surge in the garlic and onion powder.

3. Add the vegetable bouillon. Surge in the water consistently until the mix is joined and smooth. Surge in the coconut milk, soy sauce, mustard, and pepper. Add salt to taste. Continue to hotness and blend over medium hotness until

the sauce has thickened and is murmuring.

4. Add the meatballs back to the compartment and cook them for 3 minutes or until they are warmed through. Adornment with parsley and serve.

4.Vegan Southwestern-Style Chili Recipe

Cooking stew can without a very remarkable stretch be a the whole day issue, yet this vegan bean stew isn't simply simple anyway versatile.

Steadily stewing the trimmings is what all things considered gives stew its rich and overpowering person. In this equation, premade salsa, which is stacked with flavor, is used to quickly and viably duplicate the kind of bean stew that has stewed the whole day.

For best person and surface, search out a salsa that is open in the refrigerated piece of your main store rather than shocked salsa found on traders' racks, which will overall have a "creamier" surface than recently made.

This equation calls for completed vegetable protein, in any case called TVP, but if you end up with various kinds of veggie sweetheart meat substitutes accessible, feel free to utilize them or simply add more mushrooms.

On the off chance that you're not a fan of dull beans, endeavor pinto, kidney, chickpeas, or a combination of cooked beans taking everything into account.

Prep:15 mins

Cook:30 mins

Total:45 mins

Trimmings

- 1 cup TVP, sprinkled with 7/8 cup water or as instructed on pack

- 2 teaspoons oil, similar to olive or canola

- 1/2 cup cut cremini or button mushrooms

- 1/4 teaspoon fit salt

- 2 tablespoons stew powder, or 1 (1.25-ounce) group stew getting ready

- 2 (12-ounce) compartments new delicate salsa

- 1 (16-ounce) can veggie darling refried beans

- 1 (15-ounce) can diced fire-cooked tomatoes

- 2 (15-ounce) containers dim beans, exhausted and washed

- 1 cup veggie darling cheddar, optional

- 1/2 cup hacked cilantro, for serving

Headings

1. Gather the trimmings.

2. In an immense pot or shallow stockpot, add doused TVP, cooking oil, cremini or button mushrooms, and 1/4 teaspoon salt.

3. Toss well using a little spatula and a short time later cook over medium to mediumhigh hotness until TVP is sautéed and mushrooms are fragile, around 4 to 5 minutes.

4. Add heap of bean stew getting ready and cook an additional 1 second over medium hotness.

5. Add salsa, refried beans, fire-cooked tomatoes, dull beans, and cheddar (if using). Blend well to combine while cooking over medium hotness.

6. Reduce hotness to a stew and grant to cook for an additional 15 minutes, and up to 30, blending consistently to hold stew back from remaining and burning-through.

7. Remove from hotness and grant to cool quickly. Preceding serving, top with cilantro and some different trimmings you appreciate (crushed tortilla chips, guacamole, veggie lover bitter cream, etc)

Putting away and Freezing

- Store extra bean stew in an impenetrable compartment for as long as four days in the fridge.

- To freeze cooked bean stew, move it to an impenetrable cooler safe compartment and store for as long as two months in the cooler. To defrost, essentially heat over medium hotness in a pan until warmed all through.

5. Vegetarian TVP Sloppy Joes

Messy joes, the mid-twentieth century formula for sweet and tart ground hamburger sandwiches, has acquired prevalence once more, so it's no big surprise there is a meatless adaptation—veggie lovers and vegetarians need to partake in this retro formula as well. These messy joes made with TVP (finished vegetable protein), making them ideal for your veggie lover or vegetarian kids, are more grounded than standard messy joes since they're without cholesterol and much lower in fat than hamburger or even turkey.

Messy joes are fun (and muddled) to eat and are extraordinary for a group, particularly since they're financial plan cordial and simple to make. Serve these TVP messy joes with a tomato, cucumber, and corn salad and chips as an afterthought.

Despite the fact that TVP regularly should be rehydrated prior to adding to a formula, since it will stew alongside vegetable stock and pureed tomatoes, it very well may be added with no guarantees.

Prep:10 mins

Cook:20 mins

Total:30 mins

Fixings

- 2 to 3 tablespoons olive oil

- 1 onion (diced)

- 1 green or red ringer pepper (diced)

- 1 1/2 cups vegetable stock

- 2 1/2 cups pureed tomatoes

- 1 tablespoon bean stew powder

- 1 tablespoon soy sauce

- Dash of hot sauce or Tabasco sauce, discretionary

- 1 tablespoon sugar

- 1 1/2 cups TVP

- Salt, to taste

- Freshly ground dark pepper, to taste

- Hamburger buns, for serving

Guidelines

1. Gather the fixings.

2. Heat the olive oil in an enormous skillet over medium-high hotness; add the onion and chime peppers and sauté for 3 to 5

minutes or until the onions are delicate.

3. Reduce the hotness to medium-low and add the vegetable stock and pureed tomatoes, blending to consolidate well. Once hot, add the bean stew powder, soy sauce, hot sauce or Tabasco sauce, sugar, and TVP, mixing admirably to join.

4. Allow to stew for something like 15 additional minutes and season well with salt and pepper. The veggie lover messy joe combination will thicken marginally as it cools, worry don't as well in the event that it appears to be all in all too slight while cooking.

5. Taste, and change flavors if necessary.

6. Spoon the TVP messy joe combination onto cheeseburger buns.

7. Serve hot and appreciate.

6. Veggie darling Chili with Smart Ground Mock Meat Crumbles

If you like stew, attempt this "strong" veggie darling bean stew with loads of phony meat for a decent and "liberal" surface. The Smart Ground brand isn't hard to use as a cheeseburger substitute and has a meat-like surface and taste. The Smart Ground, once in a while called "veggie ground" or even "soy breaks down" tastes and behaves like ground burger—just with liberally less fat. You can sauté it in a non-stick compartment, but you may need to add a scramble of oil since the veggie ground itself doesn't contain fat like ground burger does.

This vegetarian bean stew with Smart Ground or veggie ground is both low in fat and calories, while presently giving a gigantic heap of strong veggie sweetheart protein. Note that if you use Smart Ground isolates, they are, no doubt, veggie sweetheart. Regardless, if using another brand, check the etching to research the beautifications list as not all veggie dear meat substitutes are vegan.

This recipe keeps it major using canned beans, so you skirt the time it would take to cook the kidney beans. Regardless, you could set it up using got beans on the dry possibility that you like.

Prep:10 mins

Cook:40 mins

Total:50 mins

Enrichments

- 2 tablespoons vegetable oil
- 1 (12-ounce) bundle Smart Ground Original (or other veggie darling meat substitute)
- 1 cup cut onion
- 1 cup cut green pepper
- 1 cup cut celery
- 15 ounces canned kidney beans, drained
- 15 ounces canned corn bits

- 32 ounces canned tomatoes, diced or cut

- 6 ounces tomato stick

- 2 minced cloves garlic

- 1 1/2 tablespoons bean stew powder

- 1 1/2 tablespoons ground cumin

- 3 teaspoons salt, sea salt or fit

- 1-2 cut green onions

- 1/2 cup veggie sweetheart cheddar

- 1 tablespoon sound yeast

Rules

1. Gather the enhancements.

2. Heat a colossal pot over medium hotness and add around 1 tablespoon of oil.

3. Once the oil is hot, add the Smart Ground meat substitute (breaking down it as you go in case everything's remained together), the hacked onion, cut green pepper, and cut celery. Hotness for around 2 to 3 minutes, just until onions are to some degree clear, blending now and again. Add a more perceptible extent of the oil dependent upon the situation to keep the meat substitute from remaining.

4. Add in the drained kidney beans, corn parts, canned tomatoes, tomato stick, minced garlic, stew powder, cumin, and salt,

blending to join well.

5. Once the improvements are particularly consolidated and stewing, decay the hotness to low, cover, and grant to stew for no under 35 minutes, and up to 90 minutes, blending conflictingly.

6. Taste and change the flavors.

7. Serve hot and appreciate! You can complete dishes of bean stew with cut green onions, veggie darling cheddar or sound yeast.

Vegetarian Fish Recipes

Fish are colleagues, not food! Leave them off your plate and get into one of these convincing ocean sincere vegan fish designs in light of everything.

Presumably the most startling estimation we've heard of late is the assumption that we may have fishless oceans by 2048 due to overfishing, pollution, and loss of biodiversity.

With 90% of the world's wild 'fish stocks' totally exploited due to overfishing, it's time we changed things up and stop seeing fish as a boundless wellspring of food and leave them where they ought to be – in the ocean.

Leaving our unpleasant friends alone at any rate doesn't mean we need to miss dinners we like seared fish and French fries, fishcakes, or salmon bagels in any case as there are a ton of creative ways to deal with displace fish and fish with plant-based trimmings which are better for you and the planet also.

Here is a part of our main veggie lover fish and fish designs that look and taste like the certifiable

1. Tofish and Chips

Singed fish and French fries are a praiseworthy British significant point that many appreciate on a Friday night. However, with experts expecting that we may see fishless oceans by as exactly on schedule as 2048, it's an ideal chance to dispose of the fish and quest for plant-based different alternatives.

Complete Time: Prep 20 min

Cooking 35 min

Fixings

- 280 g Naked Tofoo
- 3 Tbsp olive oil
- 300 g peas
- 3 Tbsp veggie darling crème fraiche
- 800 g potatoes like King Edward
- 1 Tbsp plain pre-arranged flour
- 100 g self-rising flour
- 1 tsp dried kelp, crumbled (optional)
- 100 ml veggie darling ale

- Oil for significant fricasseeing

Guidelines

1. Preheat the oven to 200°C/180Fan Gas 6. Channel the Tofoo and wipe it off.

2. Strip the potatoes and cut into chips, bring a tremendous compartment of tenderly salted water to the air pocket, and cook the cut potato for 5 minutes, a channel well then, toss with the olive oil. Spread out onto a non-stick warming plate and cook on the oven for 30 minutes, turning somewhat through cooking time.

3. While the chips are cooking, cook the peas in a dish of percolating water for 5 minutes, channel and tip into a food processor with the crème Fraiche, surge until especially solidified. Warmth carefully.

4. Cut the Tofoo into 4 areas and buildup in the pre-arranged flour. Torrent oneself rising flour with the kelp and add the brew, surge again until you have a smooth rich player.

5. Hotness with respect to 8cm oil in a skillet to 180°C. Take a piece of tofu and plunge in the player to cover similarly, carefully lower into the hot fat, and cook for 2 to 3 minutes, until splendid and new. Repeat with the other 3 pieces.

Serve cooked Tofish with chips and a spoon overflowing with peas, brighten with lemon wedges.

2. Vegan Tuna Sushi Bowl

This Vegan Tuna Sushi Bowl has plant-based fish made with tomatoes, and everything on your #1 hit bowls (counting the bursting mayo)!

Trimmings

- Tomato Tuna
- 3 Roma tomatoes
- 1 Tbsp new ground ginger 15 g
- 2 Tbsp soy sauce 30 mL
- 1 Tbsp toasted sesame oil 15 mL
- 1 Tbsp sriracha 15 g
- 1 tsp lime juice 5 mL

Sushi Rice

- 1 cup uncooked sushi rice 240 g

- 2 Tbsp rice vinegar 30 mL

- 1 Tbsp sugar

- ½ tsp salt

Fillings

- 1 avocado

- 2 carrots

- Nori, salted ginger, wasabi, consumed onions

- ½ cucumber

- 2 Tbsp mayonnaise vegetarian or common

- 2 tsp sriracha

Rules

1. Prep Tomatoes: Score fairly "X" in the lower part of every tomato. Drop into a pot of permeating water, requiring out after only 10 seconds, when the skin starts to strip away. In a flash dive tomatoes into a bowl of freezing water. The skin should come clearly off! Chop down the middle, discard seeds and inside parts and cut into diminished down pieces. Move to a bowl.

2. Marinade: Stir together the soy, ginger, sesame oil, sriracha, and lime juice, then, at that point, shower over the tomato. Throw to cover, and let marinate for some place close to 30 minutes.

3. Rice: Meanwhile, set up your sushi rice. Add 1 cup cold water to the rice and set over high warmth until water bubbles. Reduction warmth to a delicate stew and let cook for 15 minutes, covered. Crash warmth and let rest while you set up the remainder of the situation. Mix rice vinegar, sugar, and salt. Not long before serving, mix this into the rice.

4. Gather: Chop or sadly cut your fillings. Mix mayonnaise and sriracha. Spoon rice into each serving bowl, finishing with fillings and tomato fish.

3. Veggie lover Tofu "Fish" Sticks

The fish sticks dear by kids doesn't ought to be made using fish. For a privately evolved veggie-darling fish substitute, you can utilize tofu and ocean advancement pieces.

You need firm or extra-firm tofu for this situation. Tofu gives a critical consistency so the sticks hold their shape and don't self-destruct when warmed or seared. Moreover, nori, the consumable dried kelp, gives the ocean, ocean significant individual that makes the sticks taste like fish.

The orchestrating time for this formula is everything except for five minutes in any case contingent on the sort of tofu you use, you may require some extra an optimal chance for smashing the tofu. All around, firm and extra-firm tofu now have a piece of the drenched state cleared out yet it can't hurt setting the square of tofu between paper towels or an optimal dishcloth and with a pile on top to take out any abundance dampness. This association may require as long as 30 minutes. The drier the tofu, the better the breading will come out. Right when the sticks are breaded and the tofu is too wet, the breading will not have the firm surface that makes fish sticks a particularly spellbinding supper area for adolescents.

Possibly than utilizing egg and milk for breading the counterfeit fish sticks, this condition utilizes soy milk prepared with soy sauce for plunging before diving the sticks in a blend of bread pieces, nori, and lemon pepper.

Since the soy sauce and the ocean advancement now add sharpness to the dish, there is no essential for additional salt in this situation.

You can either warm these veggie-dear phony fish sticks in the stove, which is the lowfat technique for setting them up. On the other hand, you can sauté them.

Like guaranteed fish sticks, these are best when served hot clearly from the barbecue or the skillet.

There are different alternatives rather than how you can serve these "fish" sticks: with a veggie darling tartar sauce, ketchup, or even farm dressing or grill sauce. To make them a full weeknight supper or school year the initial shot dinner, serve them with pureed potatoes, French fries, or yam fries, and veggie sweetheart coleslaw as a touch of knowing the past. Prep:5 mins

Cook:40 mins

Total:45 mins

Trimmings

- 2 blocks tofu (firm or additional firm, squashed)
- 1/4 cup soy milk
- 2 tbsp. soy sauce
- 2 tbsp. lemon juice
- 1 cup bread pieces
- 2 tbsp. nori kelp (disintegrated)
- 1 tsp. lemon pepper

Rules

1. Pre-heat broiler to 375 F.

2. Cut tofu into strips and coat well with flour.

3. In a pie plate or shallow bowl, whisk together the soy milk, soy sauce, and lemon juice. In a substitute bowl or pie plate, join bread scraps, nori, and lemon pepper.

4. Circumspectly dunk floured tofu in soy milk blend, then, at that point, coat well in bread scraps.

5. Get ready for 40 to 45 minutes, turning over once, until firm and awesome brown. On the other hand, scorch on the various sides in a touch of oil.

4. Banana Blossom Fish Cakes

Banana bloom gives these sans fish vegetarian all around disposed of 'crab fish' cakes a superbly real flaky surface while dill and shallots add flavor. Present with a crush of lemon and hand-cut chips for a great and direct evening dinner.

Trimmings

- 1 can Cooks&Co banana blooms
- 1 can chickpeas (depleted)
- 1 Tbsp olive oil
- 2 shallots, delicately cut
- 4 cloves garlic, delicately cut
- 1 Tbsp blended flavors
- 0.25 cup finely-cut off new dill
- 2 Tbsp veggie-darling mayo
- 2 tsp Dijon mustard
- 1 cup panko breadcrumbs (without gluten if fundamental)

Headings

1. Wash and channel the canned banana grows well. In like way, wash and channel the chickpeas and put them away.

2. Finely hack the banana bloom pieces.

3. Warm the olive oil in a skillet over medium warmth. Add the cut shallots and garlic, and cook, mixing habitually, until mellowed. Add the blended flavors and cook until fragrant. Speedily discard the gleam and move to your food processor.

4. Add the chickpeas and hacked banana blooms to the food processor. Heartbeat until everything is broken into more subtle pieces. Stop to scratch down the sides depending upon the situation. Move to a blending bowl.

5. Blend in the new dill, veggie darling mayo, mustard, eventually the breadcrumbs. Taste and add more salt, pepper, and blended flavors depending on the situation.

6. Construction the cakes from two tablespoons of blend. Cautiously place the veggie dear crab cakes into the warmed oil.

7. Singe the veggie lover crab cakes for around 3 minutes for each side, or until well sautéed on the various sides and hot all through. Serve hot, with veggie dear tartare sauce and cut lemons.

5. Veggie darling Filet-O-Fish Sandwich

Veggie darling Filet-o-Fish Sandwich (McDonald's Copycat)

There are such endless sensible food assortments puts that are at long last getting with the occasions and offering stunning veggie sweetheart different alternatives (Hello Impossible Whopper!!) however horrifyingly Mcdonald's is now uncovering in and haven't figured where the world is going. Have no dread, nevertheless, because I'm here to make all of your veggie darlings' unobtrusive food dreams work out exactly as expected!

Battered and seared tofu "fish", new rich tartare sauce, and vegetarian American cheddar make this veggie sweetheart construction incredibly better contrasted with the first.

Cook Time: 45 min

Hard and fast Time: 45 min

Trimmings

- 1 14 oz bunch additional firm tofu, squeezed for 20 minutes or incredibly firm tofu

- 1/3 cup plain breadcrumbs

- 1 cup finely squashed mollusk wafers (like the careful you'd get with soup, you can feel that they are close to the saltines at the corner store)

- 2 tbs kelp granules which you can appear

- 1 vegetarian egg

- 2 cups canola oil or other high-heat oil

- 4 buns

- 4 cuts vegetarian American cheddar

- Tartare Sauce

- ¾ cup veggie darling mayonnaise

- 2 tbs sweet relish

- 1 tbs lemon juice

- ¼ tsp lemon punch

- ¼ tsp salt

- ¼ tsp new broke pepper

- ½ tsp onion powder

Headings

1. Mix the tartare sauce decorations, cover, and put in the cooler for some place almost 60 minutes.

2.   Hotness the canola oil in a tremendous critical lined skillet over medium-high warmth. Grant it to get extremely hot while you prep the remainder of the decorations. Distinguish an arranging rack over a warming sheet and set it close to the skillet.

3.   Turn the tofu block on its side and filet down the center the long way, then, at that point, filet those pieces down the center again so you end up with 4 indistinguishable portions of tofu

4.   Put ½ cup vegetarian egg (I utilized Just Egg, I tracked down that the rely upon your sense disengaged extravagantly) in a little dish at any rate sufficiently colossal to have the decision to dunk the tofu in

5.   Join the kelp, breadcrumbs, shellfish saltine pieces, and ¼ tsp salt on an enormous plate

6.   At the point when your oil is hot, dunk the tofu in the egg then into the kelp blend, cautiously at any rate immovably getting the breadcrumbs into it on all sides.

7.   Spot in oil and rehash with another piece of tofu. (Fry just 2 bits of tofu at a time otherwise it will cool the oil superfluously and the tofu will hold a huge load of oil and it will be extravagantly smooth!)

8.   Fry for 2 minutes then, at that point, flip and fry an additional 2 minutes, abstain from and place on a warming rack to debilitate. Rehash with the other 2 bits of tofu.

9.   Gather your sandwiches, spread a little tartare sauce on the

base bun, place a cut of cheddar, tofu piece, spread more tartare on the top bun and you're finished!

Vegetarian CHEESE RECIPES

Luckily, there are a lot of choices nowadays with regards to vegetarian cheddar, and probably the best are hand crafted.

On the off chance that you'd prefer to have a go at hand crafted vegetarian cheddar utilizing a formula, you're in the ideal spot!

1.Cranberry and Pecan Vegan Cheeseball

This occasion amazing vegetarian cheeseball is made with a mix of rich cashew cheddar and sweet-tart dried cranberries, all covered in a cranberry walnut outside.

Prep Time:8 hours 15 minutes

All out Time:8 hours 15 minutes

Fixings

- 1 1/2 cups crude cashews absorbed water 4–8 hours, depleted and flushed

- 1/4 cup coconut oil softened

- 2 tbsp lemon juice

- 1 1/2 tbsp water

- 1/4 tsp salt

- 1 cup improved dried cranberries isolated

- 1/2 cup slashed walnuts

Guidelines

1.   Place the cashews, coconut oil, lemon squeeze, water, and salt into the bowl of a food processor fitted with a S-edge. Mix until smooth, halting to scratch down the sides of the bowl depending on the situation. Add ¾ cup dried cranberries. Interaction just until cranberries are finely slashed and consolidated into the combination. This should take around 15 to 30 seconds, contingent upon your food processor.

2.   Transfer the cashew combination to a fixed holder and refrigerate for 3 to 4 hours, until it's firm enough to shape.

3.   Stir the walnuts and remaining ¼ cup of cranberries together in a little bowl. Eliminate the cashew combination from the cooler and utilize your hands to shape it into a ball. Press the walnuts and cranberries into the outer layer of your cheeseball, moving it in the blend in the event that you'd like.

4.   Transfer the completed cheeseball to a serving plate and serve promptly, or place in an impenetrable holder and chill until prepared to serve.

Notes

Planning time incorporates chill time and drenches time for the cashews.

2. Veggie lover Parmesan Cheese

It wouldn't be pasta night without a piling bowl of Parmesan cheddar for garnish.

Beneficial thing this vegetarian Parmesan from Yumsome prepares in a short time!

My vegetarian parmesan is ideally suited for adding a nutty, sweet-appetizing character to a wide range of dishes, in addition to it's super-simple and extremely speedy to make with only four fixings. It's without gluten as well.

Prep Time2 mins

Complete Time2 mins

Fixings

- 125 g crude Fairtrade cashews
- 3 tbsp dietary yeast drops
- ¾ tsp ground ocean salt
- ½ tsp garlic powder

Directions

1. Whizz every one of the fixings together in a food processor or blender for two or three minutes, until they look like exceptionally fine breadcrumbs.

2. Store in a sealed shut container at room temperature for as long as a half year.

3. Sound Vegan Queso

This habit-forming queso plunge from Making Thyme for Health is produced using veggies, so no concerns in case you are back for quite a long time. Sound Vegan Quesosatiny and made with nutritious fixings. Sans nut, without gluten, sans dairy, and sans soy.

planning time: 10 cook time: 20 complete time: 30

Fixings:

- 2 tablespoons additional virgin olive oil

- 1 cup diced onion (around 1/2 huge onion)

- 1/4 cup cleaved carrot (around 1 medium-size carrot)

- 3 garlic cloves, minced (around 1 tablespoon)

- 1 cup (1-inch) cubed butternut squash (or sub more potato)

- 2 cups (1-inch) cubed reddish brown potato (around 1 huge potato)

- 1 cup plain unsweetened non-dairy milk

- 3 tablespoons white vinegar

- 2 tablespoons decreased sodium tamari

- 1 teaspoon mustard powder

- 4 tablespoons healthful yeast

- 1/2 teaspoon cumin

- 1 teaspoon fine ocean salt

- 1/4 teaspoon chipotle powder (discretionary yet suggested)

- 1 (4 ounces) can dice green stews (discretionary)

Directions

1. In a huge pot, warm the olive oil over medium hotness. Add the onion and carrot and cook for 3 minutes. Mix in the cubed butternut squash (on the off chance that utilizing), potato and garlic cook for an additional 2 minutes.

2. Pour in the milk then, at that point, heat to the point of boiling. Decreased to a stew, cover with a top, and permit to cook at a low bubble for around 10-15 minutes, until the squash and potato are exceptionally delicate. You ought to have the option to squash it with a fork. Whenever it's done, put the pot away and permit it to cool.

3. After the squash combination has cooled, move it to a blender and include the leftover fixings. Mix on high until smooth. Add more milk, each tablespoon in turn, if necessary. Trial to check whether you incline toward more salt or preparing and add on a case by case basis.

4. Stir in the green chilies the hard way, in the event that utilizing, fill a bowl for serving. Enhancement with chilies, diced tomato, as well as cilantro. Store extras in a water/air proof compartment for as long as 3 days.

5. You can likewise substitute 1 cup of potato (two potatoes all out for the formula) in the event that you would prefer not to utilize butternut squash. You might have to add around 1/4 cup more milk when mixing.

6. Rice milk makes this without nut yet any non-dairy milk you like as long as it's plain and unsweetened.

7. substitute coconut aminos for a sans soy elective

8. 1/4 teaspoon chipotle powder gives this queso a gentle degree of zest. Add more in the event that you like. You can likewise utilize 1-2 tablespoons of adobo sauce from a can rather than the powder.

4. Avocado Cashew Cream Cheese

At long last something deserving of your bagel! It will spruce up a veggie sandwich as well. The varieties are interminable. Leave out the spices and garlic, attempt minced carrots and celery, minced olives, or even toss in some pecan and agave.

Fixings

- 1/2 cup crude cashews

- 1 cup water

- 1 medium avocado

- 1/4 cup lemon juice

- 1/2 teaspoon Italian flavoring

- 1/4 teaspoon granulated garlic or 1 minced clove
- salt, to taste

Guidelines

1. Soak the cashew in the water for the time being or if nothing else 2 hours.

2. Drain off any extra water that was not consumed by the cashews. Add the depleted cashews, avocado, lemon juice, Italian flavors, and garlic into a blender.

3. Blend until smooth, pause and scratch down the sides and rehash until the blend is smooth

5.Creamy Vegetable-based Vegan Cheese Sauce

This smooth sauce has the sharp kind of cheddar. It's made with a base of cauliflower, turnip, and carrots. You can utilize all cauliflower or all turnip in case that is all you have, yet I think the blend of the two preferences best.

planning time: 20 MINUTES Cook time: 15 MINUTES

Complete time: 35 MINUTES

Fixings

- 1 1/2 cups cauliflower florets

- 1 cup cut carrots

- 1/2 cup stripped and diced turnip

- 1/3 cup cashews

- about 2 1/2 cups water

- 1 cup unsweetened

- Unsweetened Almond Milk

- 1/4 cup healthful yeast

- 1 teaspoon granulated garlic

- 3/4 teaspoon salt, or to taste in case you are on a salt-limited eating routine

- 1/4 teaspoon smoked paprika

- 1/8 to 1/4 teaspoon mustard powder

Directions

1. Add the vegetables and cashews to a pot and add 2½ cups water or enough to cover the veggies.

2. Bring to a bubble, then, at that point, go hotness to medium-low and cover. Cook until the vegetables are delicate, around 15

minutes. They are done when you can undoubtedly penetrate them with a fork.

3. Pour the cooked veggies into a colander to deplete the water out. Add the depleted vegetables to your blender alongside the unsweetened Califia Farms Unsweetened Almond Milk, healthful yeast, garlic, salt, paprika, and mustard powder. You can begin with ⅛ teaspoon of the mustard powder if your family may like it milder.

4. Blend until smooth, scratch down and mix somewhat more.

5. Use over pasta, blended in with sauteed mushrooms for a portabella chez steak, or even specialist it up with Mexican flavors and make nacho cheez!

6. Slow Cooker Method: Add the vegetables and cashews to a 4-quart slow cooker and add enough to water cover the veggies. Cook on low for 7 to 9 hours or while you are away working.

7. Pour the cooked veggies into a colander to deplete the water out. Add the depleted vegetables to your blender alongside the unsweetened Califia Farms Unsweetened Almond Milk, dietary yeast, garlic, salt, paprika, and mustard powder. You can begin with ⅛ teaspoon of the mustard powder if your family may like it milder.

8. Blend until smooth, scratch down and mix somewhat more.

148

Made in the USA
Las Vegas, NV
20 November 2021